Computing with a Laptop for the Older Generation

Robert Penfold

Bernard Babani (publishing) Ltd
The Grampians
Shepherds Bush Road
London W6 7NF
Englan

D0256021

Please note

Although every care has been taken with the production of this book to ensure that any projects, designs, modifications, and/or programs, etc., contained herewith, operate in a correct and safe manner and also that any components specified are normally available in Great Britain, the Publisher and Author do not accept responsibility in any way for the failure (including fault in design) of any projects, design, modification, or program to work correctly or to cause damage to any equipment that it may be connected to or used in conjunction with, or in respect of any other damage or injury that may be caused, nor do the Publishers accept responsibility in any way for the failure to obtain specified components.

Notice is also given that if any equipment that is still under warranty is modified in any way or used or connected with home-built equipment then that warranty may be void.

© 2009 BERNARD BABANI (publishing) LTD

First Published - February 2009

Reprinted - May 2009

British Library Cataloguing in Publication Data

A catalogue record for this book is available from the British Library

ISBN   978 0 85934 702 0

Cover Design by Gregor Arthur

Printed and bound in Great Britain for Bernard Babani (publishing) Ltd

Preface

Laptop PCs have been available for many years, but until quite recently they have sold in relatively small numbers. It is easy to see why, with a typical laptop then having a mediocre specification and a high selling price. There were actually some laptops that had quite impressive specifications by the standards of the day, but were so expensive as to be well beyond the reach of the average computer user.

Today the situation is very different. Laptop computers have rapidly fallen in price, increased in specification and performance, and become much lighter in weight. They can be used practically anywhere, then stored away out of sight. It is therefore, not surprising that laptop sales now far exceed those of desktop machines and that they are increasingly becoming the machine of choice for the older generation.

You may want to use your laptop as your main computer or as an extra machine. You may want to use your laptop on the move, at home, at work or on holiday. Whatever your specific requirements are, the friendly and practical approach of this book will help you, in an easy and enjoyable way, to choose a suitable model, set it set up properly so that it is working efficiently, and then get the most from it.

This book is written in plain English and, wherever possible, avoids technical jargon. Little previous knowledge of computing is assumed, but in some sections it will be helpful if the reader knows the basic fundamentals of using a PC and the Windows Vista operating system. Much of the book also applies to Windows XP machines.

Even though this book is aimed at the older generation of computer users, it is also suitable for anyone of any age who has a laptop or is thinking of buying one.

Robert Penfold

Trademarks

Microsoft, Windows, Windows XP, and Windows Vista are either registered trademarks or trademarks of Microsoft Corporation.

All other brand and product names used in this book are recognised trademarks, or registered trademarks of their respective companies. There is no intent to use any trademarks generically and readers should investigate ownership of a trademark before using it for any purpose.

Contents

Setting up your laptop 31

Customising your laptop 67

Telephone Messages

Message for: ....

Message taken by: ....

Date: ....**Time:** ....

Caller Details:

Name: ....

Telephone number: ....

....

Reason for call:

....

....

....

....

Please call back: ☐

Other action required (please state):

....

....

◆ **Read the caller's number back**
  to them to ensure details are correct

BCS/1013/TEL12

4

Internet and security 99

Laptop basics and selection

Times past

At one time you would only buy a portable PC such as a laptop or notebook if you really needed the ability to compute while on the move. The drawbacks of mobile PCs were many, while the advantages were few. In fact there was probably only one significant advantage, which was the ability to work away from a mains power point. Even this advantage was not all it could be. The battery life of portable PCs tended to be very limited, and was often a matter of minutes rather than hours. Even if you carried a spare battery it was likely that a mains supply would soon be needed in order to carry on computing.

Apart from their portability, laptop and notebook PCs tended to compare very unfavourably with desktop PCs. Many of the drawbacks centred on the usability of portable PCs, or perhaps it would be more accurate to say that the problems centred on the lack of usability. One of the main points of contention was the poor screens fitted to most of the devices. Most had monochrome screens that were all right for basic business applications such as spreadsheets and word processing, but were of little use for things such as photo editing and most graphics applications. The lack of colour could still be something of a drawback in the more simple applications, and it was certainly a very undesirable feature. Colour screens were actually available in the early days of portable PCs, but at prices that were strictly for the "well heeled". Whether a colour or monochrome screen was chosen, its performance was likely to be quite poor in most respects.

One advantage of the LCD (liquid crystal display) screens used in most portable PCs is that they do not have the distortions associated with normal CRT (cathode ray tube) screens. A straight line is displayed as such even if it is close to one edge of the screen. Even the most expensive CRT screens tend to produce noticeable curvature when displaying this type of thing. Of course, these days many desktop PCs are equipped with LCD screens, but this was not the case a few years ago. LCD screens were little used outside the field of portable computing.

In other respects the screens of early portable PCs left a lot to be desired. The LCD screen technology meant that everything was very precise, but a lack of contrast often gave the perception of a rather fuzzy picture that lacked detail. The main complaint of most users was the very narrow viewing angles of these early LCD screens. In order to get the best results from these screens they had to be viewed from directly in front. The brightness dropped dramatically if you moved slightly out of position. With some screens it looked as if the computer had been switched off if you moved your head slightly to one side!

Another problem was that the screens were relatively dim. In direct sunlight the screen often looked completely blank. In fairness to the LCD technology of the day, a CRT screen would probably look equally blank if operated in direct sunlight. With a portable PC you expect it to operate wherever you happen to be at the time, but this is probably not being realistic. With any computer screen it is necessary to find somewhere that provides reasonable operating conditions. The real problem with the early LCD screens was that they were difficult to view in any fairly bright conditions. For those computing on the move this could make it difficult to find somewhere that the display could be viewed reasonably well.

At a price

Probably the biggest drawback of portable computers has been their price. The best portable PCs cost thousands of pounds and were not something that the average PC user could afford. Unfortunately, at the budget end of the market the prices were still relatively high. A portable PC having a specification that roughly matched a "run of the mill" desktop PC would usually cost at least twice as much, and carefully comparing the two sets of specifications would probably reveal that using the portable PC involved a few compromises.

There were various reasons for the high cost of portable PCs. Probably the main contributor to the problem was the high cost of the LCD screen. At the time, practically every desktop PC had a monitor that used an ordinary CRT, and was relatively cheap. The LCD screen of a portable PC could easily cost more than a typical desktop PC complete with its CRT based monitor. This meant that there was no way that portable PCs could compete with desktop computers on price.

Of course, many of the components in a portable PC had to be much smaller and lighter than the standard items used in desktop PCs, and this inevitably made them more expensive to produce. The fact that portable PCs sold in relatively small numbers also meant that the savings due to high volume production were not as great as with desktop PCs.

Other drawbacks

Some drawbacks of portable PCs are built-in to this type of computing, and are not easily solved by improvements in the technology. One of the big selling points of the original PCs was that they were easily expanded. In addition to adding external units via the computer's ports, there were several integral expansion slots that could take various types of expansion card. A lack of physical space means that it is difficult for a portable PC to offer much scope for internal expansion.

The keyboards of portable PCs have been a contentious issue with many users. While the keyboards supplied with many desktop PCs are of dubious quality, there is usually no difficulty in unplugging the supplied keyboard and connecting one of your own choosing in its place. This is not really an option with a portable PC, where the keyboard is normally built-into the main unit. You can add an external keyboard to most portable PCs, but using a separate keyboard is only a practical option if it will never be necessary to use the computer on the move.

With a desktop PC it is not usually too difficult to change any part of the system if you find it difficult to work with, or it becomes out of date. Even internal parts of the unit such as drives and the display card can usually be changed quite easily. The same is not true of portable PCs. This is not to say that changes can not be made at all, but in general things are less flexible with portable PCs. It is usually impossible to change some parts of the system, and changing others can be quite difficult and expensive. Modern portable PCs are better in this respect than those from a few years ago, but it is important to make sure that you are reasonably happy with the system in its original form.

Up to speed

Portable PCs have tended to lag behind desktop PCs in terms or raw computing power. The speed of desktop PCs has increased dramatically over the years, but so has the complexity of the microprocessors and other components such as the video processor. Despite improvements in the technology, this complexity has generally meant an attendant increase in the power consumption of the computer. While this increase in power consumption is unhelpful, with desktop PCs it is not a major problem. It is just a matter of equipping the computer with a bigger power supply and improving the cooling system to deal with the extra heat that is generated.

The situation is very different with portable PCs. There is no space for larger power supplies and cooling systems. This is academic anyway, since a portable PC that had a power consumption of a few hundred watts would run the battery flat in a few minutes! The need to keep the power consumption within reason has resulted in portable PCs tending to have lower levels of performance than desktop computers.

Times change

Things move on in the world in general and in the sphere of computing, and this has resulted in portable PCs becoming more competitive with desktop PCs. Many people now buy portable PCs even though they will not need to do any computing on the move, but are laptops really a practical alternative to desktop PCs? This is to some extent a "how long is a piece of string?" style question. It depends on the way in which you intend to use your PC.

Taking the speed issue first, it is probably still the case that a typical desktop PC is significantly faster than a typical laptop. However, in the past the computing power of a typical desktop PC was barely sufficient to run many of the application programs that would be installed on it. This is no longer the case, and even a budget desktop PC has ample computing power to handle standard office applications such as word processor and spreadsheet programs.

In fact a modern low-cost PC is quite capable of handling more demanding applications such as drawing, media player, and photo editing programs. Most can even do a good job with a high-power application such as video editing. The only common application where budget and mid-price PCs do not function well is some types of computer gaming.

Since the average desktop PC has a degree of overkill when used in most everyday applications, raw computing power is no longer a major issue for most users. Although a budget or mid-price laptop PC might not provide anything approaching the ultimate in computing power, it should be perfectly adequate for most applications. For gamers there are laptop PCs that have powerful processors and "state of the art" graphics systems, but the average laptop is not really well suited to playing computer games. Even these up-market specials are not really the ideal choice for computer gaming unless portability is essential.

Running costs

The cost of running a PC is something that was not a major consideration in the past. Although the amount of power consumed by a typical desktop PC was not insignificant, it was not that high either. Early PCs probably consumed about the same amount of power as a 100 watt light bulb. The monitors of the day were based on CRTs and typically consumed a bit more than the PC base unit. The total consumption was therefore quite low, as was the relative cost of each unit of electricity.

Running costs have steadily increased over the years, with electricity tending to become much more expensive, and computers becoming bigger and better. The power consumption of a modern desktop PC can easily be 300 watts or more, and a large CRT monitor probably has a power consumption that is comparable to this. In other words, using a modern desktop PC with a large CRT monitor results in a unit of electricity being used every hour or so. This makes running costs quite high even for those using a PC an hour or two per day. It makes the running costs very high for those that use a PC all day and practically every day.

The rise in the popularity of flat panel monitors is partially due to the fact that they have much more modest power requirements than the CRT variety. The LCD technology used in flat panel monitors actually requires very little power at all, and I presume that most of the power going into this type of monitor is actually consumed by the lighting unit. Even for a large flat panel monitor, the typical power consumption only seems to be about 30 to 40 watts. In other words, about a tenth of the power needed to run an equivalent CRT unit.

In fact, for those using a PC for many hours a day it makes economic sense to dispose of a CRT monitor and replace it with a flat panel unit. This gives the advantages of the more accurate geometry and generally better picture quality associated with this type of monitor, plus much lower running costs. Over a period of time the reduction in the electricity bills should more than pay for the new monitor.

Using a laptop PC instead of a desktop PC takes the cost savings a stage further. In order to obtain a reasonable battery life it is necessary for a portable PC to have reasonably low power consumption. The lower the rate at which power is drained from the computer's battery, the less likely you are to find that the battery has gone flat before you have completed the current task. In these days of expensive electricity, very low power consumption is clearly a big advantage even for users who will never use their laptop on the move.

The actual power consumption seems to vary greatly from one laptop to another, but something like 60 to 65 watts seems to be typical. Bear in mind that this is the consumption of the entire computer, including the monitor. It is therefore about one tenth of the power consumption of a typical desktop PC and CRT monitor. In comparison to a typical desktop PC plus flat panel monitor the power consumption is only about a fifth as much. You could run a laptop PC all day and all night on little more than a single unit of electricity. Running one continuously during normal working hours would only use about one unit of electricity every two days.

With such a large difference in the power consumptions of typical laptop and desktop PCs, any added cost when initially buying a laptop will be recouped fairly rapidly. In fact the total cost of ownership of a laptop PC is likely to be very much less than that of a desktop PC. Obviously the comparative costs depend largely on how much the computer is used, but assuming it is not used a few times and then put away in a cupboard for a few years, the laptop should always be cheaper in the long term.

Open options

An advantage of portable PCs that should not be overlooked is that they can be used on the move, as a home PC, or a combination of the two. Clearly a desktop PC does not provide the same degree of versatility. If you buy a laptop PC for use at home but decide to take it on holiday for playing games or DVDs on wet afternoons, you can do so. Taking a desktop PC on holiday is unlikely to be a practical proposition!

Space-saving

I suspect that the main reason for the massive rise in the popularity of laptop PCs for home use is that they require less space. The manufacturers of electrical and electronic goods seem to come up with an endless stream of new gadgets. Modern life is incomplete unless you obtain practically all of these must-have devices. Unfortunately, the rooms in our houses do not expand slightly each time a new gadget comes along.

Fig.1.1 *A modern laptop combines the base unit with the monitor,
keyboard, and pointing device*

Most desktop PCs are substantial pieces of equipment. Matters are made
worse by the fact that a conventional desktop PC actually consists of
three main units (base unit, monitor, and keyboard). In a real-world
system there are likely to be other items in the system such as a mouse
and a printer. This all takes up a substantial amount of space. The
situation can be eased slightly by using a flat panel monitor, but the
system as a whole still requires a fair amount of space.

There are PCs that are have small base units, and these are worth
considering if space is strictly limited. However, bear in mind that the
potential for internal expansion with these diminutive PCs is often limited
or non-existent. Also, even a PC based on a small base unit might take
up a fair amount of room. In other words, it is easy to end up with the
worst of both worlds when using one of these PCs. You lose much of the
potential for internal expansion, but there is no great saving in the amount
of space needed to accommodate the system.

Fig.1.2 A laptop occupies little space when the case lid is closed

A laptop PC is genuinely space-saving, since it effectively combines the keyboard, base unit, and monitor in a single unit of modest dimensions (Figure 1.1). You can use it on the kitchen table or practically any flat surface that you can find. Having finished a computing session the laptop can be folded up (Figure 1.2) and put away in a drawer or cupboard. Although the folded width and depth of a laptop PC are not particularly small, the tiny height makes it easy to find a suitable storage space. Using a laptop removes the need to have an area of a room that is dedicated to computing.

Of course, in practice it might not be as simple as that. If the laptop is used with printers and other gadgets, it is unlikely that it will be possible to store these away in a drawer or cupboard along with the laptop. This depends on the nature of the add-on devices, and in the case of printers it is certainly possible to obtain portable units that are small and light enough to be stored out of sight with the laptop. Even if one or two full-size peripherals are used with a laptop, the small size of the computer itself helps to ease problems with fitting everything into your home.

Fig.1.3 A laptop keyboard is not a standard PC type

Downside

Laptop PCs certainly have plenty of advantages for many users, but it is inevitable that there will be a few drawbacks as well. Some of these can be avoided by making sure that you buy the most suitable type of laptop. For example, a laptop that has quite a small screen is not a good choice if you will need it for graphics applications or your eyesight is not very good. Something like a 15.4 or 17 inch screen is more appropriate in either case. Anything less than a 15 inch screen is definitely not a good idea if your eyesight is even slightly below par.

For most users, actually getting information into a laptop is probably the main bone of contention. A conventional PC keyboard is something in the region of 450 millimetres wide, which most users would probably consider to be far too much for a portable PC. It is therefore inevitable that the built-in keyboards of laptop PCs are non-standard to a certain extent. In fact real-world laptop keyboards are well removed from the conventional PC variety. This is demonstrated by Figures 1.3 and 1.4 which respectively show typical laptop and conventional PC keyboards.

Of course, the standard QWERTY part of a PC keyboard is to be found on a laptop, and it is usually something close to the size of the equivalent part of a conventional PC or typewriter keyboard. The function keys will also be present, but possibly with a small amount of relocation. Beyond that, it is likely that the keyboard will only have a passing resemblance to a normal PC, or that it will be almost completely different.

Fig.1.4 The standard PC keyboard layout is too wide for a laptop PC

The non-standard nature of a laptop keyboard is just something you have to accept. The physical constraints mean that the only way of having a full-size PC keyboard would be to have a rather elaborate system of folding it up into something of standard laptop proportions. Such keyboards have been produced, but never achieved popularity. I suppose that there has to be some doubt about the reliability of any system of this type, although such worries are perhaps unfounded. Probably the main reason for their lack of success is that the unfolded laptop is relatively large, which is not very convenient for those using the unit on the move.

Most laptop PCs have provision for using an external keyboard, or have a USB port that can be used with an ordinary PC keyboard that has this type of interface. Using an external PC keyboard is an attractive proposition if you are familiar with a conventional PC keyboard and will be using your laptop at home,. There is a huge range of keyboards to choose from, so it should not be difficult to find one that suits your needs.

This is not necessarily the best approach though. Although initially you might find that the built-in keyboard is difficult to use, it is likely that you will become accustomed to it over a period of time. The same is true if you are not entirely happy with other characteristics such as the springiness of the keys. It is possible that you will never feel completely happy using the keyboard, but it is more likely that within a fairly short period you will be able to use it without any problems.

Mouse

The aspect of laptop computing that is most likely to give problems to new users is the mouse. To be more accurate, it is the lack of a mouse that tends to be a problem. In fact a mouse will probably be offered as an optional extra, or you can connect a standard PC mouse to one of the computer's USB ports. Like an external keyboard, adding a mouse is an attractive proposition if you will be using your laptop at home. You can control the onscreen pointer in the normal way, and there is no need to carefully set up any built-in pointing device.

Although it was not quite a standard feature in the past, a modern laptop PC invariably has some form of built-in pointing device, and this is usually in the form of a touch-pad. These can be a bit fiddly and awkward to use, and they can be especially difficult if your fingers are not as nimble as they used to be. If you have problems using the built-in pointing device I would certainly recommend using a mouse instead. When using the laptop at home there should be no difficulty in finding adequate space to use the mouse on the desktop. Using a mouse on the move is less convenient, but could be worthwhile if you will normally work with the laptop where it will not be too difficult to accommodate the mouse.

Price

The cost of computers in general has been steadily reducing in recent years, which is perhaps surprising considering that the specifications have been getting ever more ambitious. What were once expensive optional extras such as CD and DVD writers are now included as standard. While it is still the case that laptop PCs are more expensive than the desktop variety, the difference has narrowed in both relative and absolute terms. You can now buy good laptop PCs at prices that are very reasonable, and well within the budgets of most PC users. Consequently, price is no longer a major drawback unless you are operating on a very tight budget.

Laptop or notebook?

The terms "laptop" and "notebook" seem to cause a certain amount of confusion these days, and the differences between the two have decreased over the years. In fact the differences have been eroded to

Fig.1.5 A notebook PC on top of a notebook type. The notebook PC is slightly smaller overall, and it is also lighter, but the difference is not immediately obvious

the point that these two terms are largely interchangeable. In the past, a laptop PC was larger than a notebook type, and physically was much the same as a modern laptop. The technology has moved on over the years, and a modern laptop is better specified while perhaps being a bit smaller, but the general appearance and concept remain the same.

Notebook computers were significantly smaller than the laptop variety, but still had screens of reasonable dimensions and a proper QWERTY keyboard. This made them more portable, but made them relatively fiddly and difficult to use. Modern notebook PCs have tended to grow in size, meaning that they are now little different to laptops. In fact some manufacturers do not seem to differentiate between the two, and seem to use whichever term takes their fancy. This means that for most practical purposes there is no difference between the two any more.

A few manufacturers do produce laptop and notebook PCs, with a slight difference between the two ranges. When folded, a notebook is a bit thinner than a laptop. The difference is not usually very great, but it apparently enables notebooks to fit into special compartments in some briefcases, camera bags, etc. A chunkier laptop will not always fit into one of these cases. Figure 1.5 shows a Dell laptop PC underneath an HP notebook type. Both of these computers have 15.4 inch screens.

Fig.1.6 *A modern word processor has a WYSIWYG display and can handle graphics such as photographs*

The difference in height is not great, and there are no significant differences in the width and depth dimensions, but the notebook PC is noticeably lighter than the laptop type. Apart from the difference in size and weight there is little practical difference between the two types, although the smaller size of a notebook PC means that it is likely to have a slightly shorter battery life. In this book the term "laptop" is used to cover laptop and notebook PCs.

Choosing a laptop

When choosing any computer you need to consider the way in which it will be used, and the application programs that will be run on it. There is no point in buying a top-of-the-range laptop and then using it for nothing more than word processing or playing Solitaire. A relatively simple and inexpensive laptop can handle basic applications such as these. There is also no point in buying a very basic laptop and then trying to run high-end applications on it. Even if your application programs will run on it, they are unlikely to work in a really usable fashion.

Fig.1.7 Even the built-in Wordpad program can handle graphics

Word processing

Modern word processors are more sophisticated than the early programs for the PC that were strictly text-only and had no graphics capability. Apart from some very basic programs that are really text editors, word processors that run under Windows provide WYSIWYG (what you see is what you get) displays. In other words, the text is displayed in the correct font, style, colour, and so on. Also, these programs can handle graphics elements of various types, such as diagrams, photographs, and charts (Figure 1.6).

The demands on the hardware vary enormously depending on the type of word processing that is undertaken. Little loading is placed on the processor when undertaking straightforward word processing that does

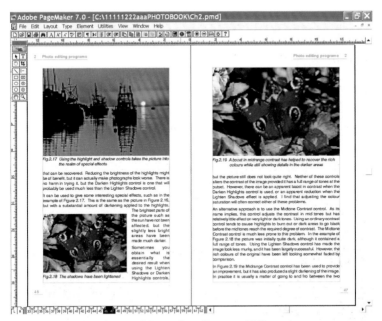

Fig.1.8 A modern laptop PC can handle most DTP work

not include any graphics content. A WYSIWYG text display requires much more processing power than a basic text-only screen, but it is something that any reasonably modern laptop should be able to handle with ease.

For this type of thing it is not even essential to buy any word processor software. The WordPad program built into Windows (Start – All Programs – Accessories – WordPad) is suitable for basic word processing. In fact you can even add graphics to the text (Figure 1.7), albeit with much less control than with an upmarket word processor. However, for anything other than fairly basic word processing tasks it is advisable to obtain some good quality software.

If a laptop is needed for taking notes, and even if large amounts of text will be accumulated, a very basic laptop should be more than sufficient. A basic laptop is also adequate for more serious word processing that has no more than a small amount of graphical content. For word processing that includes a fair amount of graphics it is probably best to opt for at least a mid-range laptop that has a fairly large screen (15 inches or more).

DTP

DTP (desktop publishing) software has similar requirements to the word processing variety. A significant amount of word processing work actually entails using the program as a sort of pseudo DTP type. The difference between these two types of program has become blurred in recent years. In general though, DTP programs provide more control over page layouts and require a bit more processing power and memory in order to run really well. Figure 1.8 shows the Adobe PageMaker program in operation.

Using a DTP program to do page layouts that only contain text is not very demanding on the hardware, and any reasonably up-to-date laptop should be able to handle it. More complex DTP work that involves a significant graphical content requires a more upmarket laptop. This means at least a mid-range unit with a 15-inch or larger screen, a minimum of 512 megabytes of memory, and preferably 1024 megabytes of memory when using Windows XP, and double these figures when using Windows Vista.

Business applications

Other standard business applications such as databases and spreadsheets do not require a particularly powerful PC. Bear in mind that the use of graphics will place higher demands on the processor. Some types of graphics require a reasonably large screen, but in other respects any laptop should be able to handle standard business programs.

CAD

CAD stands for computer aided design or computer aided drawing, and it is software primarily used for producing technical drawings (Figure 1.9). This usually means a plan for something, such as a house extension, some house wiring, a piece of electronics, or an item of furniture. Producing two-dimensional drawings is not demanding on the processor, but a large screen is needed when producing complex drawings. A 15 to 17-inch screen is adequate for many types of drawing, so a laptop with a large screen is just about suitable for some two-dimensional CAD work.

Three-dimensional CAD is far more processor intensive than the two-dimensional variety, particularly if the program is designed to give very realistic looking results. This type of thing almost invariably requires a

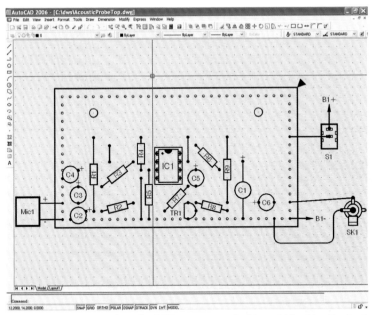

Fig.1.9 A laptop can handle CAD programs, but is not ideal for the task

very large screen. Consequently, it is an application where even an upmarket laptop could prove to be inadequate. In fact a laptop is less than ideal for most CAD work. Unless portability is essential, this is one application where a desktop PC will normally be a much better choice.

Internet

There seems to be a popular misconception that a fairly powerful PC is needed in order to surf the Internet. This is possibly due to the slightly dubious advertising used by some PC manufacturers when the Internet really started to become popular. It was sometimes suggested that a powerful PC would give quicker and more reliable surfing, which is not really the case. In this context the speed and reliability is largely dependent on the speed and quality of the Internet connection. A fairly modest laptop PC should be perfectly adequate for surfing the Internet, even when using a fast broadband connection.

It is not even essential to have a large screen in this application. Many Internet sites seem to be optimised for quite low screen resolutions such

Fig.1.10 A modern laptop can handle photo-editing, but one having a large display is preferable

as 640 by 480 pixels or 800 by 600 pixels. Few require anything beyond 1024 by 860 pixels. Most laptop PCs can handle screen resolutions of this order. Any laptop having a screen size of 14 inches or more should certainly be able to do so.

Photo editing

The increase in the popularity of digital cameras has resulted in a similar rise in the popularity of photo editing programs such as Photoshop (Figure 1.10), Photoshop Elements, and Paint Shop. Programs of this type mostly require a fairly high screen resolution, so a laptop having a resolution of at least 1024 by 860 pixels will probably be required. A screen size of 15 inches or more and a somewhat higher resolution is preferable.

The amount of memory and the processor power required for photo editing depends on the nature of the images that will be processed. Low-resolution images for use on the Internet are not very demanding in either respect. The same is not true of high-resolution images of the

Fig.1.11 Windows Media Player can be used to play DVDs

type produced by most modern digital cameras. A mid-range or upmarket laptop having a suitably large screen should do very well in a photo editing application where high resolution images are involved. At least 512 megabytes of memory will probably be required for good results with Windows XP, and 1024 megabytes is preferable. About double these amounts are needed when using Windows Vista.

Multimedia

With desktop PCs there are specials that are primarily designed for use in multimedia applications. There are also fancy media PCs that are designed to blend into the average living room rather better than a typical desktop PC. Last, and by no means least, there are laptop PCs that are primarily designed for multimedia applications. These used to be supplied with the Windows Media Edition operating system instead of the standard version of Windows XP. These days the Home Premium version of Windows Vista is a popular choice for the operating system. Laptops that have a suitable specification sometimes have a media oriented version of Windows available as an optional extra. Note that these laptops often provide something less than a full implementation of the features available from Windows Media Edition. You have to carefully read the "fine print" in order to ascertain whether all the facilities you require are actually included.

A multimedia laptop is the obvious choice if you require a portable PC that will mainly be used for multimedia applications. On the other hand, one of the non-portable media PCs might be a better choice where portability is not important. One of these units should have a full implementation of the facilities supported by the operating system, or something very close to it. As already pointed out, multimedia laptop PCs sometimes have significant gaps in their specifications.

Bear in mind that practically any modern laptop PC s should be capable of playing MP3 and other audio files, as well as audio CDs, DVDs, and movies in AVI, WMV, and the other popular formats. Obviously the specification must include a DVD drive of some kind if you will need to play DVDs, but these are now included as standard with many laptops. Some only have a CD writer as standard, and it is worth paying for an upgrade to a DVD writer even if you are not much interested in multimedia applications. The higher capacities of DVDs when compared to CDs means that they are much better suited to backing up your hard disc drive and data. These drives can be used to read and write CDs as well.

In most cases you will not have to buy any software for playing media files. The built-in player of any modern version of Windows can handle many requirements, including playing DVDs (Figure 1.11). Free players such as Apple's iTunes can handle most additional requirements. There might be other multimedia software bundled with the computer, so it is worth checking to see if there are any useful extras of this type. Unfortunately, many of the programs bundled with new PCs are some form of trial software that only runs properly for a limited period, or are cut-down versions of the full programs. You have to pay the appropriate sums of money in order to get the genuine articles. It is well worthwhile investigating any genuinely free software bundled with your PC.

Games

As pointed out previously, most laptop PCs are not well suited to playing computer games. I suppose that their suitability is to some extent dependent on the types of game that you will be playing. Things like Solitaire, old "classic" action games, and puzzles do not usually require a great deal of computing power and high-speed graphics cards. The latest games with high resolution animations of almost photographic quality do require a top-notch graphics card and processor.

Of course, most of the latest action games can be run at lower resolution and with fewer colours, and the demands on the hardware are then much reduced. Consequently, a mid-range or top-end laptop should be able to handle most games, but not necessarily in a form that will be to your satisfaction. This type of laptop should be adequate if you are happy with something less than optimum graphics quality, as many people are.

There are a few laptops that have potent processors and fast three-dimensional graphics cards, and these are specifically aimed at those requiring a good games performance from a mobile PC. No doubt these work very well, but they should as they are very expensive. Large amounts of computing power tend to consume similarly large amounts of power, so a powerful laptop can reasonably be expected to have a very large battery and (or) a short battery life.

Bear in mind that laptop PCs lack the internal upgrade and expansion potential that can be taken for granted with desktop PCs. Upgrading a laptop games computer by (say) fitting a new graphics card is unlikely to be possible. A complete new laptop will almost certainly be required if you decide that your laptop is a year or two old and can no longer handle the latest games releases to your satisfaction.

Second-hand?

There is a thriving market for second-hand PCs, and the current popularity of laptop PCs means that there is a particularly buoyant second-hand market for this type of PC. Unfortunately, this is not good news from the buyer's point of view. Strong demand means high prices, and bargains are hard to find. While I would not go as far as to say that you should never buy a pre-used laptop computer, I would generally recommend buying a new one if at all possible.

Modern laptops are mostly quite powerful PCs that are very capable, and even the lower cost types will run most PC software. As already pointed out, they are not well suited to all types of software, but they will run most programs in a usable fashion. The same is not true of many laptop PCs from a few years ago. One of the more upmarket laptops from that period will no doubt still give good results today provided it is in reasonable order, but the lower and mid-range units might be found wanting.

Before buying a second-hand laptop it is definitely a good idea to make comparisons with new budget units. When making the comparison, bear in mind that the new unit should last several years longer than the second-hand laptops.

Check to see what software, if any, is supplied with the pre-used PC. It could end up costing more than a new laptop if the latter is supplied with lots of good bundled software while the former is supplied with little or no software. You are in luck if things are the other way around and the second-hand laptop is supplied with lots of extra software that was not included in the deal when it was new. Also check that a second-hand laptop is supplied with any essential accessories such as a battery and mains adaptor/charger. Another point to note is that replacement batteries for laptops can be very expensive, and usually are. Make sure that a second-hand unit is supplied with a battery that is in good condition, and ideally is should come complete with a new battery.

Specifications

In many respects the specifications of laptops are no different to those of desktop PCs, and if you understand one then you understand the other. There are some important differences though, and these are discussed in the following sections. For the benefit of those who are new to computing, some general information about PC specifications will also be provided.

Clock speed

On the face of it, the clock speed of the processor used in a PC should give a good guide to the speed of the PC itself. In practice matters are not as simple as that, and for a number of reasons it is not safe to assume that a PC having a clock speed of (say) 2.6 gigahertz is twice as fast as one that is clocked at 1.3 gigahertz. The main reason for this is that there are several processors currently being used in laptop computers, and these have totally different designs. Some require more clock cycles than others for a given task.

Even when comparing two computers that have the same make and type of processor, clock speed is not a totally reliable guide to the speed of the computer as a whole. There are other factors that govern the operating speed of a computer. They generally exercise far less control over the operating speed than the processor, but their influence can still be very significant. The speed of the graphics card is crucial when any complex graphics is involved, especially when the graphics is of the three-dimensional variety. In fact this is one instance where the speed of the processor could be of secondary importance.

The amount of memory fitted to the computer is also an important factor. In general, the greater the amount of memory fitted, the faster it will run most software. However, these days most PCs are equipped with a substantial amount of memory as standard. This is something where the laws of diminishing returns apply, and using a larger amount of memory will not necessarily make a great amount of difference to the operating speed. On the other hand, performance will certainly suffer if a small amount of memory is used.

Another factor that can be of significance is the chip set that is used to support the processor. The chip set provides things like the input/output ports, and generally helps the processor to communicate efficiently with the memory and other parts of the PC. Some chipset and processor combinations work better than others.

Where high performance is essential you really need to read reviews of any laptops that are of interest. These are fairly easy to find on the Internet, and they are also to be found in computer magazines. Any review should include a speed test that shows how well the laptop as a whole compares to some other computers when running various types of software. This enables the relative speeds of the computers to be assessed in a realistic fashion.

Screen

The size of a monitor or television screen is its diagonal measurement. In the case of a monitor or television that is based on a CRT it is not the true diagonal measurement. CRTs tend to have rounded corners, and the size measurement is based on the tube having notional square corners. In other words, the quoted screen size is greater than the actual diagonal measurement of the display area. In specifications for CRT monitors you will sometimes find the visible or usable screen size quoted, and this is the true diagonal measurement of the screen.

Laptop PCs use LCD screens that have perfect geometry, so the notional size and the actual diagonal measurement are the same. A 14-inch LCD screen is equivalent to a CRT screen size of a little over 15 inches, and a 15-inch LCD screen is roughly equivalent to a CRT screen size of about 16 inches or so. A 14 or 15 inch LCD monitor does not give a particularly large viewing area by current desktop PC standards, but it is good enough for most purposes. As most modern software works best at quite high screen resolutions, I would suggest opting for a screen size of 15 inches or more. A large screen is also very helpful for those with eyesight that is substantially less than perfect.

Viewing angle

One advantage of CRTs is that they are bright when viewed at virtually any angle. The same is not true of LCD displays, which give optimum brightness when viewed from precisely in front. As pointed out previously, a huge drawback of the early units was that they rapidly dropped in brightness when viewed even slightly away from the optimum position. Also, the colours then tended to become oversaturated unless the picture was viewed from something close to the optimum position. This made it almost impossible for two people to simultaneously view the screen properly.

Modern LCD screens are much better, but there is still a significant reduction in brightness if the screen is viewed off centre. Some screens perform much better in this respect than others. The monitor I am using while writing this piece gives very little change in brightness even if I move well off centre. My other LCD monitor is far less accommodating.

The viewing angle gives an indication of how far you can go off centre before the brightness and general display quality significantly degrades. The vertical and horizontal viewing angles are generally different, and so they will usually be specified separately. A high viewing angles is better than a small one, but there is more to display quality than the viewing angle. Screen quality is a very subjective matter, so ideally you should see a laptop in action and try it for yourself before actually buying it.

Native resolution

An LCD screen is designed to operate at a specific screen resolution, which for many 14-inch screens is 1024 by 768 pixels. This is known as the native resolution, and it is the highest that can be used. It is the setting that will provide the best results in most applications, but it can sometimes be advantageous to switch to a lower screen resolution. For example, some games give smoother action if set for a lower screen resolution. It is usually possible to use at least one or two lower resolutions, but these inevitably involve some compromises and might not give quite the picture quality that you would expect. It is not possible to use a resolution that is higher than the native resolution.

Battery life

There are two versions of the battery life parameter. The batteries used to power laptop PCs are of the rechargeable variety, and using primary cells is not a practical proposition as the running costs would be too high. One version of the battery life figure is the number of times that the battery can be recharged before it degrades and will no longer hold a charge properly. This figure is usually the minimum number of charge/discharge cycles that will be provided. The battery will typically last much longer than this figure would suggest provided it used in accordance with the manufacturer's recommendations.

The other version of the battery life figure, and the one that is of more practical significance, is the time that a fully charged battery can run the computer before it has to be recharged again. The power consumption of a laptop PC varies considerably depending on the task being undertaken, so this version of the battery life figure tends to be something of a guesstimate. It should therefore be taken as nothing more than a general guide.

The power consumption of laptop PCs is very high by the standards of battery powered equipment. Despite the fact that the batteries are quite large, the typical battery life is only two or three hours. An extra battery is costly, but it has to be regarded as essential when computing on the move.

PCMCIA/PC Card

PCMCIA stands for Personal Computer Memory Card International Association, and it is the type of expansion slot/card used with many laptop PCs. As its name suggests, it was designed as a means of using memory cards with computers. In practice it has only been used to a significant degree with laptop computers and other portable electronic gadgets, and has never been used very much with desktop computers. Also, its use has spread to accommodate a wider range of applications than additional memory. These days PCMCIA cards are used in applications such as wi-fi adaptors, advanced sound systems, and to provide additional ports.

The original PCMCIA name has been largely dropped now. Various alternative names have been used, but PC Card seems to be the one that has gained the most widespread acceptance. Since there are now some alternative types of expansion card, you need to take due care to obtain one of the right type for your laptop.

Fig.1.12 The PCMCIA slot is above the two USB ports

These days there is often the choice of using a USB port for expansion purposes rather than fitting a PC card. The advantage of the PC card method is that the card fits right into the PC, and effectively becomes part of it. A USB add-on is an external unit that either connects to the computer via a lead, or plugs straight into the port and protrudes on one side of the laptop. Therefore, a PC card is generally the better choice for a laptop that will be used on the move. It avoids the need to plug anything into the computer and remove it again each time you set up the computer and pack it away again. Using a PC card has little or no advantage where a laptop is used as a home or small office computer.

Most laptops that use this type of expansion have one PC card slot (Figure 1.12), but a few have two. Probably only a fairly small percentage of laptop users ever need even one expansion slot. It is possible to obtain laptops that are equipped with things such integrated wi-fi adaptors and Firewire ports. It is only necessary to add them via an expansion slot if you buy a laptop that lacks these features initially.

Ideally you should assess your requirements before buying a laptop, and where possible select one that has everything you require built-in. It is then likely that there will be no need for any expansion slots during the working life of the computer. However, there will still be at least one slot available to accommodate future developments or changes in your requirements.

ExpressCard

There are alternatives to PC cards, and some manufacturers are now starting to use these instead of PC cards. Whether this is strictly necessary is debatable. Although the PC card system has its origins many years ago and it is getting "a bit long in the tooth", it is nevertheless capable of handling most requirements. It also has the advantage of being well established, which means that it is possible to obtain a wide range of cards that use this technology.

Fig.1.13 An ExpressCard expansion slot

Anyway, it is advisable to check that there is a reasonable range of matching expansion cards available before buying a laptop that has something other than PC card slots. ExpressCard is a new expansion card system that might eventually replace the PC card system. The technology is different, so the two types of card are totally incompatible. Physically, ExpressCards are about half the size of PC cards, and will normally be significantly lighter than PC cards as well. Figure 1.13 shows an ExpressCard slot in a laptop PC.

Sound

Like many other aspects of modern computing, the audio capabilities have grown enormously over the years. The original PCs were fitted with a loudspeaker, but there was no proper hardware to drive it. The purpose of the loudspeaker was to generate simple "beep" sounds. Most modern PCs still have this internal loudspeaker, and it produces a "beep" or two just after the PC has been switched on. This indicates that the built-in test routine has found nothing wrong. If an error occurs, either a different set of "beeps" will be produced, or there will be no sound from the internal loudspeaker.

These days it is the norm for sophisticated audio circuits to be integrated with the main electronics of a PC, although soundcards are still used where even greater sophistication is required. It is unusual for the loudspeakers to be built into a PC. Instead, it is used with stereo headphones or an external multi-channel loudspeaker system. The situation is rather different with laptop PCs where there are usually built-in stereo loudspeakers. There should still be at least one audio output socket that enables headphones or an external loudspeaker system to be used. There will usually be a microphone input as well, so that the unit can be used with a headset for VoIP, voice recognition, or recording notes.

Do not expect a laptop PC to have the advanced audio facilities that are commonplace with desktop PCs. In particular, any form of surround sound operation is very rare in laptop computers. Having a true surround sound speaker system built into a laptop PC is not really a practical proposition, although a few have extra speakers that give a sort of pseudo surround sound effect. Surprisingly perhaps, very few laptop PCs have built-in audio circuits and output sockets to permit their use with an external surround sound speaker system. This could be a slight drawback for those intending to use a laptop as a home computer.

Ethernet

Networking will probably not be of great importance where a laptop is the only PC you will use, but it is increasingly common for homes to be equipped with more than one computer. It is also increasingly common for some form of broadband Internet connection to be used. The normal method of networking PCs is via an Ethernet port (Figure 1.14). It is possible to directly link two PCs via their Ethernet ports, but this is a non-standard method that tends to be a bit problematic in practice. The more normal and successful approach is to connect the two PCs, together with any others in the network, via a device called a router.

Many laptop computers are used away from the home or office, and must be synchronised with a PC each time the user gets back to base. In other words, new data on the laptop must be transferred to the desktop PC, and it might also be necessary to transfer new data on the desktop PC to the laptop. There are various ways of copying the data from one PC to another, and using a network is certainly one of the most convenient. It can also be used to provide a way of linking the laptop to other hardware in the system, such as a printer and a modem that provides a broadband Internet connection.

Wi-fi

Wi-fi provides the same basic function as an Ethernet link, but using a radio link rather than connecting wires. It is effectively a wireless Ethernet link, but it is significantly slower than the wired version. This can result in quite long transfer times when dealing with really large amounts of data, but for most purposes the speed of a wi-fi connection is perfectly adequate.

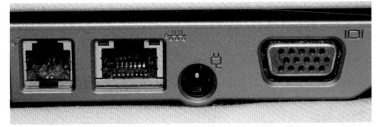

Fig.1.14 The Ethernet networking port (the second port from the left)

Wi-fi is just about ideal for use with a laptop, since it avoids the need to mess around with any connecting cables when linking and disconnecting the computer from the network. You simply place the laptop anywhere within the operating area of the base unit, switch on the laptop, wait while the operating system boots and makes the connection to the base unit, and then access the network. It depends on the coverage of the base unit, but in most cases the laptop and the base unit do not have to be placed particularly close together. You can probably sit in the garden and still access the network.

Another way of using wi-fi with a laptop is to gain access to the Internet while away from home using so-called wi-fi "hotspots". This is basically just some form of broadband Internet connection and a wi-fi base unit placed in any convenient public place. Anyone having a wi-fi equipped laptop can use the hotspot to obtain an Internet connection. This service is sometimes provided at no charge, but in most cases you have to pay for access and obtain a password before the Internet can be accessed.

The importance of Ethernet ports and wi-fi facilities clearly depends on the way in which the laptop will be used. For many it is essential to have one or the other, but it is obviously pointless if you will never have any need to connect the unit to any form of network, or a broadband Internet connection that requires this type of port. Most laptops are supplied with an Ethernet port as standard, but a wi-fi facility is likely to be an optional extra.

Note that it is possible to add a wi-fi facility to practically any laptop, so there should be no real difficulty if you purchase a laptop that lacks this facility and later on find that you need it. Provided there a spare expansion slot or USB interface it is just a matter of buying and fitting the appropriate type of wi-fi card. If you buy a laptop that is complete with a wi-fi facility it is possible that it will be provided by an expansion card rather than being genuinely built-into the computer. Having built-in wi-fi circuits is preferable since this method leaves the expansion slot free for other purposes.

Docking station

Many portable devices have some form of docking station as an optional extra. Laptop computers are no exception, but there is not necessarily a dedicated docking station available for every model. There are plenty of these units that are intended for use with practically any laptop PC. Docking stations for laptops are less popular than they were a few years ago, and relatively few users bother with them these days. The basic idea of a docking station is to give some form of expansion to the unit when it is used back at base. The laptop fits into the docking station, which then provides it with additional features.

The main purpose of docking stations with the early laptops was to provide conventional expansion slots. This enabled the laptop to be used more like a desktop PC when it was used back at base, with (say) some extra ports and a special facility of some kind provided by a couple of normal PC expansion cards. The docking station would probably provide a few other facilities as well, such as a standard PC keyboard and mouse.

I suppose that the usefulness of docking stations has decreased as the specifications of laptop PCs have become more impressive. The added expansion potential of a docking station is of little use to most users, since the basic specification of the laptop is perfectly adequate for their requirements. A docking station has a hub that provides several USB ports from a single USB port on the computer. With the USB ports of the hub connected to a mouse, keyboard, printer, scanner, or whatever, you simply have to connect the docking station to one USB port of the laptop in order to use it with all the peripheral devices. Some docking stations take things a stage further, with the USB connection being used to provide other types of port and not just additional USB types.

Further upmarket there are expensive docking stations that provide a huge range of ports, battery charging facilities, a loudspeaker system, and so on. These are usually dedicated to one particular laptop PC or range of PCs, and are not available for all laptops. The actual facilities provided by these units vary considerably from one to another. In between these two extremes there are general docking stations that connect to the laptop PC via a USB port, and provide it with serial, parallel, and PS/2 ports, and possibly some others as well. One of the more upmarket docking stations could be a worthwhile proposition provided you really need the extra facilities it provides, such as serial and parallel ports.

Setting up
your laptop

Don't panic

Traditionally, PCs are supplied in one huge box, but on opening that box you find it contains at least three more boxes. Fortunately, things are more straightforward with a laptop PC, which is not in the usual format of three main units plus a mouse. Having the base unit, monitor, keyboard, and mouse merged into one small unit helps to keep the clutter to a minimum, which is why many people opt for a laptop instead of a desktop PC.

Of course, the box will almost certainly be much larger than the laptop itself. Looking at the box you could probably be forgiven for wondering if it really contains a portable computer. Of course, the added bulk is largely padding to protect the computer on its long journey from the factory to your front door. The box should also contain at least a few accessories plus their packaging, which result in further bulk.

As a minimum there should be at least one battery and a charger/mains power supply unit. There should be at least one CD or DVD containing the operating system, and there will often be discs containing various bundled application and utility software. There might be some leads, such as one to connect the laptop's audio output socket to a hi-fi system, or one to connect the laptop's built-in modem to a standard BT telephone socket. What, if anything, you get beyond that depends on the make and model of PC that you have purchased, and whether you bought any optional accessories.

A desktop PC, unless it is primarily intended for business use, it is almost certain to be supplied with an amplifier and loudspeakers. A laptop PC is unlikely to be supplied with external loudspeakers as standard, but it will probably have built-in stereo speakers. The small size of the built-in speakers inevitably limits their sound quality. This makes them far from ideal when using the computer to listen to music.

*Fig.2.1 An inkjet printer is probably the most popular computer
peripheral*

Carrying a decent set of external loudspeakers around with you is not a
practical proposition, but any laptop PC should have a socket for stereo
headphones. These should provide much better audio quality than the
built-in speakers, and are clearly well suited to mobile operation. A set
of headphones might be included with the laptop. If not, any headphones
intended for use with portable audio players should work well with a
laptop PC.

Modern PCs, laptop or otherwise, are often marketed as systems that
contain various peripherals that would once have been very expensive
optional extras. These usually offer good value for money and make it
relatively easy for a complete beginner to buy and set up a computer
system. You are unlikely to get a laptop as part of a huge system, but
you still have be careful to avoid buying a system that contain expensive
items that you are unlikely to find useful.

An inkjet printer (Figure 2.1) is probably the peripheral that is most
frequently bundled with laptop PCs, but digital cameras and scanners
are sometimes included as well. The so-called "all-in-one" units are also

popular as bundled items. These act as a printer, scanner, and photocopier, and sometimes have a fax facility as well. If you need all the facilities provided, I suppose that one of these multifunction devices is a good adjunct for a laptop PC. Like the laptop itself, a multifunction device crams a great deal into a small amount of space.

Although very popular at one time, docking stations for laptop PCs seem to be something of a minority interest these days. This is probably due to the fact that the basic specification of the computers is much higher, which reduces the need for a unit that gives increased expansion potential. Anyway, even if you do obtain a docking station with your laptop, it is a good idea to ignore it initially. Get the laptop set up and working properly on its own first, and then go on to set it up with the docking station.

Discarding

It is tempting to throw away the box and other packaging as soon as the computer has been unpacked. This is not necessarily a good idea though. Retailers and manufacturers generally prefer faulty items to be returned complete with all packaging. Apart from other considerations, this helps to keep everything safe during the journey back to the shop or factory. It is particularly important to keep the packaging if the computer has been purchased via mail order. Using the original packing should ensure that the computer remains undamaged if it should be necessary to return it.

Of course, the packaging is unlikely to be of any further use in cases where the computer is covered by some sort of long term onsite maintenance contract. It should then be safe to discard it all at the earliest opportunity. However, check through all the packing materials very carefully before throwing them away, just in case they contain a small accessory that you have overlooked.

Positioning

With a desktop PC you have to give some thought to the positioning of the computer beforehand, rather than waiting until it arrives. The same thing really applies if you will be using a laptop as a home or small office PC. When using a laptop away from home you generally have to operate it anywhere that provides a reasonable working environment. It is a case of "beggars can not be choosers", and you just have to put up with things like the odd awkward reflection on the screen, or slightly cramped working conditions.

Fig.2.2 Make sure that you have a multi-way mains adaptor if your PC
will be used with peripheral gadgets

You have to be more particular when using a PC at home, since you will probably spend a fair amount of time sat in front of it. It will be difficult to use the computer if the working conditions are mediocre or poor, and you could soon find yourself suffering from various aches, pains, and strains. This is definitely a case of "prevention is better than cure", and it is something that should be taken seriously.

It is not a good idea to position the computer opposite a window. Although monitors have anti-reflective coatings to reduce reflections from the glass screen, no coating approaches complete effectiveness. The coatings on most flat panel monitors are actually quite good, but with the monitor facing a window it is likely that parts of the screen will be very difficult to read during daylight hours. In fact much of the screen could be impossible to read on really bright days.

Also avoid having the PC itself, or any part of the system, close to a radiator or heater. Laptop PCs are designed to have low power consumptions, and they consequently generate less heat than desktop PCs. On the other hand, they still generate a fair amount of heat, and lack ventilation systems of the type built into desktop PCs. Like desktop

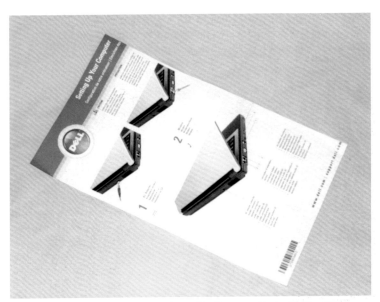

Fig.2.3 Find and read any Quickstart leaflet supplied with the PC

PCs, they need to be positioned where they will keep reasonably cool. Feeding them with additional heat is asking for trouble. When the system is installed and operational, never cover or in any way hinder the flow of air through any ventilation grilles. Doing so could easily result in costly damage to the equipment and could even be dangerous.

Modern laptop PCs often have plenty of black or dark grey plastic on the exterior, which usually looks very stylish, but does have a practical drawback. With the sun shining on the computer it can get very hot. As far as possible, use a laptop PC that has a black or dark case where it is out of direct sunlight.

A laptop will be powered direct from the mains supply when used as a home computer, making the battery unnecessary unless the computer will sometimes be used in (say) the garden. Ideally the computer system should be positioned reasonably close to a mains outlet. Having the computer and the monitor combined into a single unit means that only a single mains outlet is required in order to supply power to both of them. Of course, further sockets might be needed for major peripheral devices such as printers and scanners. If extra mains outlets will be required, make sure that you have a four or six way mains adaptor (Figure 2.2) ready when the computer arrives. You can then get straight on with getting everything set up and installed properly.

Unpack carefully

When you first receive any new gadget there is a temptation to rush in and get it unpacked and operational as quickly as possible. With something as complex as a PC this is definitely not a good idea. It needs to be unpacked and set up carefully. Unpacking the PC itself is unlikely to pose many problems, but there are sometimes bits of cardboard that

have to be carefully removed from the externally accessible disc drives before they can be used. The screen of the monitor might be covered by a translucent plastic sheet that has to be removed before it is used.

The system should be supplied with an instruction manual that gives details of any obscure bits of packing that must be located and removed. These days most computer equipment

Fig.2.4 As supplied, the head of a scanner is often locked

is supplied complete with a "Getting Started" booklet, "Quick Start" sheet, or whatever, that includes information of this type (Figure 2.3). Always have at least a quick read through any documentation of this type. A laptop PC is relatively straightforward, so there might not be anything vital in the guide. On the other hand there could be some crucial information, and a quick initial check might avoid unnecessary problems later on. It might even prevent you from making an expensive mistake.

If the system includes a printer or scanner it is virtually certain that these will have some odd bits of packing material that must be removed before trying to use the equipment. Scanners and printers have moving parts that are usually locked in place during transit. They are often held in place by bits of cardboard, plastic, foam material, and the like. These are often hidden somewhere inside the equipment. Some units, and scanners in particular, have a proper locking mechanism that must be released prior to use (Figure 2.4).

It is very important to carefully read the documentation supplied with the system, and to remove any bits of concealed packing material, undo locking mechanisms, or whatever. An attempt to use the equipment without doing so is likely to result in problems such as chewed-up bits of packing material getting into the mechanism, fuses "blowing", etc. The equipment could easily become damaged, and the guarantee is unlikely to cover this type of thing.

Cover up

Most of the packing material will be pretty obvious, but non technical people sometimes have problems with the computers ports and plugs that connect to them. The plugs on computer leads are often supplied with transparent or translucent covers that must be removed before the plugs can be fitted into the connectors on the PCs. Be careful not to overlook the transparent type. Some of these covers tend to be easily missed unless you actually look for them.

The ports on the PC are sometimes hidden behind some form of cover. One purpose of these covers is to protect the ports during transit. They can also help to keep dust out of the ports when they are not in use. The simplest type is just a plastic cover that plugs into a port. These are simply pulled free to reveal the port, but it is advisable to leave them in place until the port is required. It is advisable to keep these covers so that they can be put back in place on a port that will not be used for some time.

The more elaborate covers are built into the case of the computer and typically slide to one side and reveal several ports. It is advisable to slide the cover into the closed position when the laptop is on the move. Unless none of the ports are actually used it will probably be necessary to have the cover in the open position the rest of the time.

Checking the contents

Computer manufacturers have checking procedures which should ensure that you receive everything that you have paid for, right down to the smallest of accessories. Mistakes can occur though, so you need to check that there are no missing items as soon as everything has been unpacked. It is now standard practice for a check list to be included in the box, and this should list the laptop itself plus any items of significance that are supplied with it.

It is unlikely that a major item such as a mains charger/adaptor will be omitted, but things such as software discs, leads, adaptors, and documentation do get omitted from time to time. Carefully check that each item listed is actually present, including any seemingly minor items. Some of these might not seem to be of great importance, but you might find that somewhere down the line their absence brings things to a halt. Act at once if you are unlucky and something is missing.

Any large accessories purchased with the laptop will almost certainly have their own box and check list. It will therefore be necessary to do separate checks for any items such as printers and scanners. The check list should include a section that tells how to make a claim for missing items. Legally it is the responsibility of the retailer to supply any missing items. You will usually get the speediest result by taking the system back to the shop if you bought the item locally.

Retailers sometimes suggest that you cut out the middle-man and make a claim direct to the relevant manufacturer. Depending on the nature of the problem, this might be quicker than getting the retailer to sort things out. However, you are under no obligation to do so. The retailer has supplied unsatisfactory goods and it is their responsibility to put things right, but use a little common sense here.

Power

Once everything has been unpacked it is time to start connecting everything together. Computer systems usually have quite a number of cables to connect, which can make things a bit confusing at first. Matters are much easier with a laptop PC because the keyboard, monitor, and pointing device are integrated with the main unit. With a charged battery installed it is possible to use the computer without connecting it to anything.

Probably not for long though, because the battery will soon run flat and will have to be recharged. These days, rechargeable batteries mostly seem to be supplied in an almost discharged state. Therefore, the battery will have to be charged before the computer can be used in earnest. This is something where it is essential to read the instruction manual and follow the manufacturers recharging procedure precisely. Modern rechargeable batteries are much tougher than those of a few years ago, but there will probably be some guidelines that have to be followed in order to ensure a long operating life. Replacement batteries tend to be quite expensive, so you have to treat them with respect and make them last as long as possible.

You might have to install the battery, but it is often supplied already fitted to the computer. In some cases it is not only preinstalled, but is not actually removable by the user. In general, it is better to opt for a laptop where you can replace the battery yourself, and the vast majority of laptops are of this type. With some laptop PCs the battery is recharged by removing it from the PC and then fitting it into the charger unit. The latter might also be the computer's mains adaptor, or there could be a separate adaptor.

The modern trend is for the battery to be left inside the computer and recharged from a combined charger and mains adaptor. This is again something where it is necessary to read the instruction manual, or perhaps consult the "Quick Start" guide, to determine how battery recharging is accomplished with your particular laptop. As is often the case with equipment that uses a rechargeable battery, it is almost certain to take much longer to recharge the battery than it does to run it down. The usual way of working is to recharge the battery overnight. This should provide more than enough time to fully recharge the battery even if it is completely exhausted to start with.

It is possible that the manufacturer will state that the battery is supplied in a fully charged state. In theory, it is then just a matter of installing the battery and using the computer, or simply switching on if the battery is preinstalled. It is unlikely to be as simple as that in practice though. There could have been a gap of weeks or even months between the new laptop leaving the factory and you switching it on. The battery is almost certain to have largely run down during this time. You will then have to recharge it before using the computer, regardless of what the instruction manual may say.

Battery changing

There may never be any need to remove the battery from the computer if you only have one battery, it is preinstalled, and it is charged while in the computer. It will otherwise be necessary to remove and reinstall a battery from time to time. Most laptop batteries are quite large, and are rather like elongated digital camera batteries (Figure 2.5).

Fig.2.5 The batteries for laptop PCs are, by necessity, quite large

The battery has to be held firmly in place, but it is unlikely that a screwdriver will be needed in order to remove the cover from the battery compartment. There could well be a double catch mechanism though, as in the example of Figure 2.6. The first catch has to be slid to one side before the second one can be operated and the cover can be removed. Refer to the instruction manual if there are any problems in removing the cover, and do not try the brute force approach.

Make a note of the battery's orientation before removing it from the compartment. It is highly unlikely that it will be possible to fit the battery

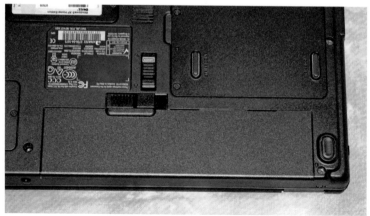

Fig.2.6 The battery compartment door is often secured by a double catch system

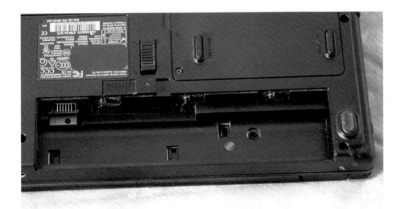

Fig.2.7 The open battery compartment with the battery removed

the wrong way round, but installing a battery it is quicker and easier when you know the correct orientation. With the cover out of the way and the battery removed (Figure 2.7), the new battery can be installed. Try to avoid touching the electrical contacts of the battery or the battery compartment. Doing so can lead to corrosion on the contacts and a poor electrical connection. The current drawn from the battery is quite high, which means that a really good electrical connection between the battery and the computer is essential.

Getting connected

In real world computing it is normally necessary to connect a PC to various external devices, even if it is a laptop type. A laptop has a built-in keyboard and pointing device, but as pointed out previously, there are advantages in using an ordinary mouse whenever possible. For the home laptop user an external keyboard could also be worthwhile. Both are offered as optional extras for most laptop PCs.

There is a port that is specifically designed for use with a mouse, but there will not necessarily be a port of this type on a laptop PC. Some mice are designed for use with a USB port, and it is a mouse of this type that is more likely to be supplied with a laptop PC. A keyboard also has its own special port, but once again, some are designed for use with a USB port, and it is more likely to be a USB keyboard that is supplied with a laptop PC.

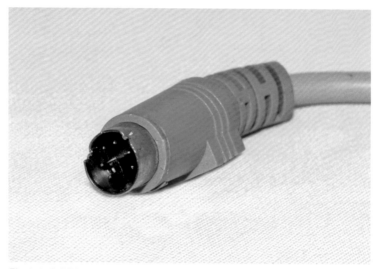

Fig.2.8 A PS/2 connector

A USB port is a general-purpose type that can be used with a wide variety of peripherals, including large devices such as printers and scanners. Most modern desktop PCs have several of them. Physical constraints mean that there are likely to be fewer USB ports on a laptop PC, but with a modern type there will probably be at least two of them, and probably more.

It is easy to tell which type of mouse or keyboard you have, since the standard keyboard/mouse connector looks very different to a USB type. The original PC keyboard connector was a large 5-way DIN plug, but this type of connector has not been used with PC keyboards for many years. It has been replaced by a miniature version, as shown in Figure 2.8. The new type of connector is usually called a PS/2 type, as it was first used on IBM's PS/2 range of PCs.

The original mice connected to a serial port of the PC, or to a port provided by a special expansion card. Both of these methods are obsolete and have not been used on new PCs for a number of years. As explained previously, modern PCs have a port specifically designed for use with a mouse. Rather unhelpfully perhaps, the mice that are used with this port also have a PS/2 connector. Consequently, there is nothing to prevent users from getting the mouse plugged into the keyboard port and the keyboard connected to the mouse port.

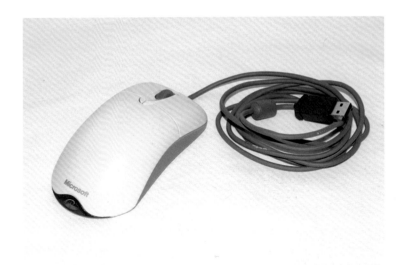

Fig.2.9 Modern mice are mostly of the USB variety, like this one

Getting the mouse and keyboard connections swapped over is unlikely to cause any problems, but it is best not to put this type of thing to the "acid test". Modern PCs, keyboards, and mice have the connectors colour coded in order to make it obvious which device connects to each of the sockets. In fact a number of the connectors used on modern PCs have this colour coding in an attempt to avoid confusion and errors when installing a new computer system.

In the case of the mouse and keyboard, they are respectively a light green colour and mauve. Consequently, there should be no real danger of getting them swapped over. Just fit the plugs into the sockets of the same colour and everything should be fine.

A mouse or external keyboard supplied with a laptop PC is likely to be of the USB variety, and these are easily distinguished from the conventional PS/2 types because the two types of connector are totally different. A typical USB mouse is shown in Figure 2.9, and a close-up of the USB plug is shown in Figure 2.10.

You need to be aware that some keyboards and mice are of the so-called "wireless" variety. Normally the mouse and keyboard are powered from the PC, but this is clearly not possible if there is no connecting cable from the PC to the keyboard or mouse. Wireless peripherals are

Fig.2.10 A USB connector is much flatter than the PS/2 variety

usually powered by one or two AA or AAA cells. A set of batteries should really be included with the system, but in practice this will not necessarily be the case.

The connection from the computer to the keyboard or mouse is provided by an infrared or radio link. Both methods require a receiver that is connected to the appropriate port or ports of the PC, usually via a short cable. Some receivers connect to a USB port while others connect to one or both of the PS/2 ports. A connection diagram should be supplied with the equipment, but it should be possible to determine which type of port is used by looking to see what type of plug is used on the receiver. It will almost certainly be a USB type.

Which USB port?

In general, it does not matter which USB port is used for a given peripheral, since all the USB ports of a PC are identical. There are actually two types of USB port, which are the original (USB 1.1) and the new high-speed version (USB 2.0), but it is very unlikely that your PC will have a mixture of the two. Unless you buy a second-hand laptop it will certainly have USB 2.0 ports. These can be used with any USB devices, including USB 1.1 types. Of course, things work at the old USB 1.1 speed if you use a slow peripheral with a high-speed USB port. With anything like this the system is always limited to the speed of the slowest part of the system.

If you are using an older PC that has USB 1.1 ports, it will work with most USB 2.0 devices, but some will not operate at all without the additional speed of a USB 2.0 port. Other units will work with an old USB port, but more slowly and not necessarily in a worthwhile fashion. Neither a keyboard nor a mouse requires high-speed operation, so both should work perfectly well with any USB port.

It is worth bearing in mind that the Windows operating system might get confused if you do not use the same port each time you use a particular USB device. Windows might consider that the device is a new piece of hardware if you connect it to a different port. The "new" hardware will then be installed by Windows. This does not matter too much, but you can end up with each device installed in Windows several times as several different pieces of hardware. This is not generally considered to be a good idea, and it can certainly make troubleshooting difficult if something goes wrong. It is preferable to always use the same port for each USB peripheral.

Finding the ports

Modern PCs are not exactly short of ports, with a number of them on the rear panel, and probably a few more at the front. Laptops are generally less well equipped in this respect, but there should still be plenty of ports scattered around the case. Do not expect the ports to be grouped together in desktop PC fashion. The small size of a laptop means that there is little space available to accommodate the ports. Laptop PC designers do their best to have the ports placed ergonomically, but they are constrained by the practicalities of the situation.

You should soon get used to things, but initially it will probably be necessary to do a little searching to find the ports you need. The actual ports present vary somewhat from one laptop to another. A typical complement would be something along these lines:

USB ports (Figure 2.11)

As already pointed out, these are the computer's main means of communicating with major peripheral devices such as printers and scanners, and they can also be used with things like keyboards and mice. The flat shape of the connectors means that they are easily distinguished from the other types of connector. There should be at least a couple of USB ports, and there should preferably be three or more. The USB ports of a laptop are entirely standard both physically

Fig.2.11 This laptop has three USB ports

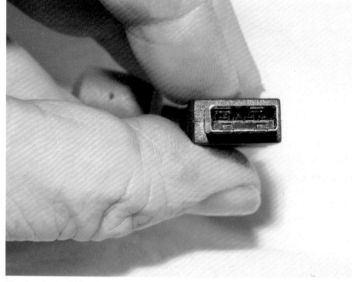

Fig.2.12 A USB plug has one half solid and one half hollow

Fig.2.13 *USB ports have a complementary hollow and solid arrangement*

and electronically. You can therefore make the connections to major peripherals using an ordinary (A – B) USB cable. Smaller peripherals mostly have a built-in USB plug or lead that connects to a laptop's USB ports in the normal fashion.

"It does not fit" is a common complaint when newcomers to the world of computing try to connect everything together. The computer manufacturers' help lines apparently receive numerous calls from the owners of new PCs who can not get one item or another connected to the base unit. An important point to bear in mind is that the orientation of plugs is often important. There are exceptions, such as the miniature jack plugs that are often used in computer audio systems, but in most cases a plug will not fit if it is upside-down, or even if it is rotated a few degrees from the correct orientation. A USB connector certainly has to be fitted the right way up.

The correct orientation often becomes obvious if you look carefully at both connectors. If you look at a USB plug you will see that it has one half solid and the other half hollow (Figure 2.12). The connector on the PC has a complementary arrangement that makes it impossible to fit the plug upside-down (Figure 2.13).

If it is not possible to see the connector on the PC properly, just try the plug one way, and if that fails, try the opposite orientation. The "hammer and tongs" approach is not the right one with electronic equipment, and attempting to force plugs into sockets is likely to damage something. A

*Fig.2.14 A modem port. This is for a dial-up connection and not a
broadband type*

plug will fit into a socket once the orientation is correct. It will not fit into
a socket properly if the orientation is not correct, and shoving a bit harder
will not change that fact. It might damage one of the connectors though,
and this type of thing is unlikely to be covered by the guarantee. New
connectors are notorious for being a bit reluctant to fit together, but some
wiggling and no more than firm pressure is more likely to be successful
than using brute force.

Note that there is a potential lack of compatibility between the USB ports
of a laptop and some USB peripheral devices. A USB port can supply
power to a peripheral gadget, but the amount of power that could
reasonably be drawn from a laptop PC is quite low. Consequently, a
laptop could be unable to operate with some USB gadgets that draw
their power from the PC. There should be no problem with low power
devices such as keyboards and mice, but some scanners and other
larger devices could fail to work. An error message to that effect will
normally be produced on the screen if a USB device tries to draw too
much power from the port.

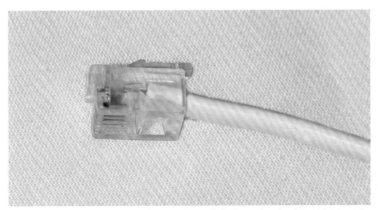

Fig.2.15 The plug on a modem lead has a lever that unlocks it from the modem port

There is a way around this problem in the form of a powered USB hub. The basic function of a USB hub is to enable several peripheral gadgets to be used with a single USB port on a computer. A powered hub includes a power supply that enables the hub to provide the full quota of power to each of its USB ports with no power being drawn from the computer.

Modem port (Figure 2.14)

Most laptop PCs have a built-in modem, but note that this is a standard 56k dial-up type and not one for use with any type of broadband Internet connection. The port connector on a laptop is usually a miniature telephone type and not a BT telephone connector. Leads to connect this type of port to a UK telephone socket are readily available from computer stores, but a suitable lead will almost certainly be supplied with the computer.

Note that there is a small lever on the plug that connects to this port (Figure 2.15). This is part of a locking mechanism that operates automatically when the plug is inserted into the modem socket. The lever must be pressed in order to release the plug so that it can be removed from the socket. Forgetting to press the lever before pulling the plug free is a common way of damaging these plugs, which are mostly of rather lightweight plastic construction.

RJ-45/Ethernet Port (Figure 2.16)

An Ethernet port is sometimes referred to as an RJ-45 port, which I think is a reference to the type of connector used. Anyway, this interface

Fig.2.16 An RJ-45 Ethernet port

enables the laptop to be connected to a standard PC network. It is also used for some types of broadband Internet connection. RJ-45 connecting cables use the same type of connector at each end, and can be connected either way around. There are two main types of RJ-45 cable,

Fig.2.17 An RJ-45 plug is a locking type with a release lever

Fig.2.18 Many laptops have a standard 15-pin video output

which are the straight and crossover varieties. Straight cables are used for most networking connections. The crossover type is used when two computers are directly linked via their Ethernet ports, rather than being connected via some form of router.

Like modem plugs, the Ethernet variety have a lever (Figure 2.17) that must be operated before the plug can be disconnected from the socket. Although Ethernet and modem connectors look similar, they are in fact totally different and incompatible. The Ethernet connectors are significantly larger than the modem variety.

Video (Figure 2.18)

Although a laptop PC has a built-in monitor, it seems to be standard practice for a video output socket to be included. This is usually a standard 15-pin (HD15) analogue type that is compatible with any normal PC monitor. The more expensive flat panel monitors also have a digital input that can be used with a DVI video output (Figure 2.19). This type of

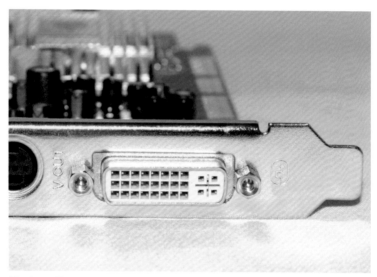

Fig.2.19 Few laptop PCS have a DVI video connector

video connector is becoming more common on desktop PCs and will probably replace the HD15 type in due course. It is still relatively rare on laptop PCs, but will probably take over from the HD15 in due course. The digital video signal of a DVI interface can provide better picture quality that the analogue signal of an HD15 interface. Consequently, where the computer and the monitor both have a DVI interface, these should be used to provide the link between the two units.

Firewire/IEEE 1394 (Figure 2.20)

Firewire, which is also known as an IEEE 1394, is a high speed serial port that was originally designed to accommodate the high data rates associated with high quality digital video. It is still in widespread use with digital video cameras and other digital video equipment. In the past it was mainly associated with Mac computers, where it was effectively the Mac equivalent of the USB ports on PCs. Many PCs are now equipped with Firewire ports as standard, or have them available as an optional extra. Firewire is now used as a general purpose port, and it is not restricted to digital video applications.

Firewire ports are only included as standard on some of the more upmarket laptop PCs, and it will not necessarily be available as an optional

Fig.2.20 4-pin (left) and two 6-pin (right) Firewire ports

extra on budget and mid-range units. Consequently, you have to be careful to choose a suitable laptop if you really must have one that is equipped with this type of interface. There are actually two types of Firewire port, which are the full six-pin type, and the smaller four-pin variety. Both types are shown in Figure 2.20.

The only difference between the two is that the six-pin type includes a power supply output that enables peripheral devices to be powered from the computer. Four-pin Firewire ports lack the supply outputs, and peripheral devices that use this version must have their own power source. There are Firewire leads that enable four-pin peripherals to be used with a six-pin computer port, or vice versa. However, bear in mind that using a six-pin peripheral with a four-pin computer port will only work if the peripheral does not need to draw power from the computer.

It is a bit unrealistic to expect a laptop PC to supply power to a peripheral device. Accordingly, the Firewire ports on laptop PCs are almost invariably of the four-pin variety and will not work with peripherals that need to draw power from the port. A four-pin port is all that is needed for a digital camcorder and most Firewire devices, but it is best not to take anything for granted and check that any Firewire gadgets you have are compatible with four-pin ports.

Fig.2.21 The power port of a laptop PC

Power port (Figure 2.21)

A laptop PC would in some ways be neater and easier to use if the mains power supply unit was integrated with the main unit. Possibly some laptops do indeed have integrated power supplies, but I have not encountered one of this type. Messing around with external power supplies seems to have become an essential part of modern life, and every household seems to accumulate a fair number of them. I have a drawer containing more than a dozen, and there are several more scattered around the house.

With many types of equipment an external adaptor is the only realistic way of handling things, but with a laptop it would probably not be too difficult to integrate the power supply with the main unit. However, this would mean carrying the extra weight of the power supply around with you even if you did not intend to power the computer from the mains supply or recharge the battery. An external power supply is cumbersome and a drawback when using a laptop as a home computer, but only a minor one.

A fair amount of electronic equipment is damaged each year by people accidentally using the wrong adaptor. In the likely event that you have a number of these units, make sure that you always use your laptop with

Fig.2.22 A USB serial port adaptor

the right one. There are probably protection circuits in all laptop PCs, but it is still possible that using the wrong mains adaptor could result in a lot of expensive damage.

Legacy ports

These are ports that were once used as the main means for a PC to communicate with peripheral gadgets such as modems and printers. However, these days there are more modern ports available for this type of thing, such as the USB and Firewire types. Consequently, these older ports are now little used and will ultimately be phased-out altogether. Serial, parallel, and game ports are still found on some desktop PCs, but they are not included on modern laptop computers.

There is obviously a problem if you have an old peripheral with a serial or parallel port that you wish to use with your laptop PC. Wherever possible it is probably best to replace the peripheral with a modern device that has a USB port. There is a potential solution in cases where it is not practical to replace the peripheral gadget. It is possible to obtain adaptors that enable serial or parallel devices to be used via a USB port. A USB

Fig.2.23   The audio output socket is primarily intended for use with headphones

serial port adaptor is shown in Figure 2.22. These do not work well in all situations, but in most cases a unit of this type will permit the peripheral to be used with your laptop PC. Some of the more upmarket docking stations provide several legacy ports, and one of these could be the best solution if more than one type of legacy port is needed.

Bear in mind that getting an old gadget connected successfully to a PC and actually getting the computer to work with the gadget are two different things. There are several potential problems, but the main one is that the old gadget will only work with a new PC if there is suitable driver software available. Driver software for older versions of Windows is usually of no use with the current versions. Most manufacturers of PC peripherals do not produce modern drivers for use with older equipment that they consider to be obsolete.

Audio output (Figure 2.23)

This is one respect that a laptop PC is likely to be much more straightforward than a desktop PC. The latter usually has at least three audio sockets, and these days there can be half a dozen or more. A laptop PC is unlikely to have more than three audio sockets, and many have just two. As a minimum there will be an output and an input. The output is likely to be optimised for the types of headphone often used with portable audio devices such as MP3 players, but it should work satisfactorily if connected to active loudspeakers of the type normally used with PCs. Results will probably be acceptable if the audio output is connected to a hi-fi system.

Fig.2.24 The audio input socket will normally work with a microphone

Audio input (Figure 2.24)

The input socket is most likely to be a microphone input. PC microphone inputs tend to be a bit problematic. One reason for this is simply that there are several types of microphone in common use, and an input that is suitable for one type will not necessarily work properly with other types. Another problem is that the original SoundBlaster microphone input was a mono type that included a supply output to power an old-fashioned carbon microphone (as used in old telephone handsets).

Some modern sound systems still have this type of microphone input, although these days it would be used with a modern electret microphone. Some modern PC sound systems have a stereo microphone input and no supply output. These are suitable for dynamic microphones, or for electret types that have a built-in battery. Finding out which type of microphone will work with a given PC is usually a matter of trying the "suck it and see" method.

Fortunately, this is academic for most PC users. Unless you wish to use a voice recognition program or record speech using your PC, it is unlikely that you will need to bother with a microphone. If you obtain a voice recognition program it will probably be supplied complete with a headset that includes a microphone. With luck, you can just plug this into the appropriate pair of sockets and it will work.

While it is not exactly a standard item of equipment, some laptops are supplied with a headset that includes a microphone, or it is available as an optional extra. Figure 2.25 shows a headset that is intended for use with a PC. Many of the microphones used in these headsets incorporate

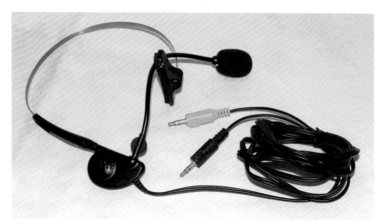

Fig.2.25 A headset for use with audio ports

noise cancelling that is intended to combat general noise in an office, and any noise from the PC.

One can reasonably expect that a headset supplied with a laptop will be properly matched to its audio system, and that the microphone will work without any problems. The plugs on headsets intended for PC use are often colour coded so that they match the corresponding connectors on the rear of the PC. Unfortunately, this colour coding is often absent from laptop PCs. The PC's instruction manuals should indicate the correct method of connecting a headset, but no damage should occur if you adopt a "suck it and see" approach.

Note that some of the more upmarket headsets do not connect to the audio connectors at all. Instead, they connect to the PC via a USB port. Headsets of this type (Figure 2.26) often have some integral digital processing that is intended to give better results with speech recognition programs. Anyway, it will be obvious if the PC is supplied with a headset of this type, since it will be fitted with a USB connector, or it will have an adaptor that has a USB connector.

Media PC audio

There are laptop PCs that are designed specifically for media applications, and it would seem reasonable to expect a laptop of this type to have the extra audio outputs needed for some form of surround sound speaker system. At the time of writing this anyway, few media laptops do actually have these extra outputs. Some have several built-in loudspeakers that

Fig.2.26 A USB headset does not use the audio ports

are designed to give a sort of pseudo surround sound effect, but still only have a standard stereo output.

Possibly this situation will change in the near future, and some current media laptops do indeed have the additional audio outputs needed for operation with a surround sound loudspeaker system. Anyway, the plugs on the speaker system will almost certainly be colour coded. The connectors on a desktop PC are also colour coded, and Figure 2.27 shows a typical set of colourful ports. Unfortunately, it is far from certain that those on a laptop PC will be colour coded. Knowing the colour coding will at least make it easy to identify the plugs of the speaker system. With luck, both ends of the system will be coded, and it is then just a matter of fitting each plug into the socket on the laptop of the same colour. These are the colour codes used for standard audio connectors in a PC sound system:

Function	Colour
Microphone	Pink
Loudspeaker	Orange
Line output	Lime green
Line input	Light blue

Computers that have some form of surround sound audio system will have some or all of these outputs in addition to or instead of some of those listed above:

Function	Colour
Front loudspeakers	Lime green
Side loudspeakers	Grey
Rear loudspeakers	Black
Central/bass loudspeakers	Orange

For the record, a system of colour coding is used for all the ports of a desktop PC. This is known as the PC 99 system. Although the norm for desktop PCs it seems to be used to a much lesser extent on laptop PCs where it is often a case of black being used for every port. Anyway, these are the PC 99 colour codes for the non-audio ports:

Port	Colour
USB port	Black
PS/2 Mouse port	Green
PS/2 Keyboard port	Purple
Monitor port	Blue
Serial port	Teal/turquoise
Game port	Yellow-orange
Parallel port	Burgundy

Assembly

So far it has been assumed here that the laptop will be supplied fully assembled apart, perhaps, for having to install the battery. It is possible but unlikely that a small amount of assembly will be required before the laptop is ready for use. Any upgrades to the basic specification, such as extra memory for example, will usually be supplied preinstalled. With

Fig.2.27 The ports of desktop PCs are normally colour coded, but this feature is usually lacking on laptop PCs

modern laptops, upgrades such as this usually require the unit to be opened up, and they are not the type of thing with which the average user will ever get involved. In some cases they have to be installed at the factory when the laptop is built.

It is possible that an upgrade that involves an expansion card will be supplied as a card that you have to install yourself. This is not too difficult and it is covered in detail in a later chapter. However, anyone not familiar with simple computer hardware upgrades would probably be well advised to get the retailer to fit the card whenever possible.

There is a slight possibility that some mechanical assembly will be required, but it is far more likely that the laptop itself will be supplied fully assembled with no odd bits of plastic to attach anywhere. The same is not true if you obtain one of the more elaborate docking stations. This may well require a bit of home assembly, but it is unlikely to be any more difficult than other gadgets that arrive as a kit of parts. As always, read the instructions carefully, do not be in any hurry, and assemble the unit in the correct order.

The big moment

With everything connected up correctly, a charged battery installed in the computer or a mains adaptor connected to the power port, you are ready to switch on and boot into the operating system. If there are several peripheral devices connected to the computer it is probably as well to do one final check to ensure that everything is plugged in correctly. Are all the plugs fully pushed into their ports on the laptop and making reliable connections? Even experienced computer professionals have been known to spend quite some time troubleshooting a new PC before they realise that it is not receiving any power. If you are using the mains adaptor, is it plugged into the mains and is the mains outlet switched on?

The system of on/off switching used for laptops is exactly the same as the one normally used with desktop PCs. Switching the computer on is accomplished by operating a pushbutton switch, which is often to be found on the keyboard near the function keys. It is not usually too difficult to spot, but if in doubt its position should be indicated in the relevant sections of the instruction manual and the Quick Start Guide.

These days computers are supplied with the operating system preinstalled, and there will usually be some bundled software as well. Therefore, when you switch on the computer it will go through the usual start-up and boot routine and go into Windows. Unfortunately, the first time you boot into Windows it is likely that there will be a certain amount of setting up to do, but this is usually just a matter of answering a few simple questions.

The exact routine varies depending on the make and model of computer, and the software that is bundled with it. Consequently, it is only possible to give some general guidance here rather than precise information. The documentation supplied with the computer should give all the guidance you will need, and there is often an information sheet that goes through the setting up procedure on a screen by screen basis.

Getting Windows running is not usually the main problem. Many new PCs, whether they are desktop or laptop types, are supplied with some preinstalled application software. Some of this software is usually fully functioning, and will prove to be very useful. For example, the ever-popular Microsoft Works office suite is often bundled with new PCs, and no doubt it is found to be extremely useful by many users. Few, if any, would object to having this type of software preinstalled on their PC.

Some other types of software are more contentious. This is something that depends on the make of computer that you buy, but it now seems to be the norm for various trial programs to be preinstalled on new PCs. These are programs that are limited in some way, or "crippled" programs as they are often termed.

A program of this type will typically work in every respect but with inoperative Help and printing facilities. Another ploy is to have a program that runs normally for (say) 30 days after you first run it, but then refuses to run at all. In a similar vein, many PCs seem to be supplied with preinstalled security suites that can be kept up to date without charge, but only for a few weeks or months. The normal subscription fees then apply.

The main objection to the bundled trial software is that it can make it difficult to get the computer set up and ready for use. You would like to get into the Windows operating system and start computing, but you find that the bundled software tries to get you to go through all sorts of setting up and registering processes. There may be no way of totally bypassing these processes, and it could be necessary to take a certain amount of time going through the setting up procedures. Understandably, this gets many users more than a little narked.

It is worth bearing in mind that the computer manufacturer is paid fees for including this type of bundled software on their PCs. In effect, the cost of you new PC is being subsidised slightly by the producers of the bundled software. Another point to keep in mind is that no manufacturer will preinstall any form of spyware, adware, or anything that hides on your hard disc drive and can not be removed. Any bundled software can be removed if you do not need it. The correct methods of removing unwanted software are covered later in this book.

Therefore, you can simply go through any unavoidable setting up procedures, and then remove the offending software if it is genuinely of no interest to you. It is not actually essential to remove bundled software that you will not use. Removing unwanted software has the advantage of freeing some hard disc space, although the amount that is liberated will not necessarily be that worthwhile.

There is a slight risk that removing software, even if it is done correctly, will mess up the operating system. This is far rarer than it was in the past, with modern versions of Windows being rather more robust than those of yesteryear. Also, the applications programs and their uninstall programs are more reliable and less likely to damage the operating system.

Windows has a facility known as System Restore which can take the computer back to its previous state if something goes wrong when uninstalling software. There is no guarantee that System Restore will always be able to live up to its name, but it further reduces the risk. However, there is still a slight risk of software removal causing a problem that can not be fixed easily. Those who are not confident at using Windows facilities such as System Restore might prefer to take the safe option of leaving the unwanted software in place.

You will probably not consider this to be an option if a program keeps producing pop-up messages to the effect that you need to renew your subscription, register it, or something of this nature. It might be possible to go into the offending program and disable the messages via an Options or Preferences window, but this is not always possible. Another possibility is to alter the Windows start-up settings so that the program can not run automatically, but it is probably easier and safer to simply uninstall it.

Problems

Modern electronics is generally very reliable, but faults can occur and you might be unlucky. A modern computer is so complex that it is probably that bit more likely to go wrong than something more basic such as an MP3 player or a radio. Anyway, before taking up the matter with the retailer it is a good idea to check that the problem is not due to a minor problem or mistake that can be easily solved.

If the laptop is doing nothing at all, is it actually getting any power? Where the unit is being powered from the mains adaptor, is the latter plugged in properly, is the mains supply switched on, and is the adaptor plugged into the computer properly? The higher wattage mains adaptors, as used with laptop computers, often have an indicator light. Does this switch on when the adaptor is plugged into a mains outlet. Multi-way mains boards can be a bit temperamental. If you are using one of these to provide additional outlets, trying using a different mains socket on the panel or plug the adaptor straight into the wall socket.

There is probably a fault in the computer or the adaptor if power is definitely getting through to the adaptor and then to the computer, but the computer fails to respond properly. Computer help lines tend to receive large numbers of calls from customers who have been unable to switch on their desktop computers. They press the button on the front as per the instruction manual, but nothing happens. The problem is that they have failed to realise that there is a conventional on/off switch at the back of the computer, and that it is set to the "off" position. It is unusual for a laptop computer to have a conventional on/off switch, but it would be as well to check this point in the instruction manual. It might save some embarrassment later on!

If the computer is being run from a mains adaptor, try powering it from the battery instead. It is likely that the mains adaptor is faulty if the computer can be powered from the battery but not the adaptor. Similarly, it is likely that the battery is a dud or is not being charged correctly if it is possible to power the computer from the mains adaptor but not the battery. Did the battery go through the recharging procedure correctly, with the indicator lights switching on and off at the right times, or whatever?

It can sometimes take a few attempts to get a new battery to go through the charging process properly.

It is possible that a little investigation will find the problem and that there will be a simple solution. If not, there is no point in spending large amounts of time searching for the cause of the problem. You must contact the retailer at once if it proves to be impossible to get the computer to power-up and boot correctly after looking for any obvious problems. It is the responsibility of the retailer to sort out any genuine faults, and not yours.

Initial testing

Assuming the computer will boot into Windows, you should then try to give everything a quick test. For example, will the CD/DVD drive read and write using the appropriate types of disc? Does the sound system work correctly, do any peripherals such as a keyboard and mouse function correctly, and so on? If you can find a way of testing any part of the computer, then do so.

If there are any faults, then you need to find them and get them rectified as soon as possible. You should certainly try to avoid the situation where you do not use (say) a port until you have had the computer for some time. If you then find that it does not work properly it is possible that the computer will be out of warranty, and you will have to pay for the repair or get by without the faulty port.

Any problem found might be of the hardware variety, and very obviously of the hardware variety. For example, a CD/DVD drive door that jams, or a mouse that is mechanically faulty. It is then a matter of returning the faulty item to the retailer.

In other cases the cause of the problem might conceivably be in software, such as a faulty driver program or an incorrect setting in Windows. For example, a CD drive that reads data properly but does not play audio discs is probably functioning correctly. The lack of audio is almost certain to be caused by a software problem such as an incorrect setting in Windows or a player program that is not set up correctly.

The retailer will probably have a help line of some sort, and they might be able to provide an easy fix for the problem. If you are having problems with a faulty set-up, then it is likely that everyone else that has bought that make and model of PC will be having the same problem. With anything like this the retailer or manufacturer should soon come up with a solution which should then be available from any relevant help lines.

Note that some of these help lines are not free, or have "strings attached" such as only being free for a limited period. You should not really have to pay for information that helps to get a faulty product working properly. If a computer fails to work properly you are not obliged to use an expensive help line. You can, for example, take it back to the shop and get them to fix the problem. Where the computer is covered by an onsite maintenance contract you should be able to invoke the contract and get someone to fix the problem at your premises, and free of charge. Many computer manufacturers and the larger retailers have web sites with a support section, and this will usually have details of any common problems and suitable fixes.

Turn off

It is not unknown for Windows to boot up correctly, but to give problems when you try to switch off the computer. Sometimes you end up going around in circles and never actually manage to shut down Windows. The more common alternative is that Windows starts to go through its closing down procedure, and it normally gets close to the end, but at some point it stalls and the computer is not switched off. This problem is less common with Windows XP and Vista than it was with some earlier versions of Windows, but it can still happen.

The instruction manual for your computer should include details of how to switch it off if none of the normal methods work. This often involves holding down the On button for a few seconds. Directly switching off the hardware is not usually to be recommended, since it tends to leave a number of temporary files on the hard disc drive. These files are deleted by the operating system when the computer is switched off in the normal way. However, Windows XP and Vista are less easily fazed by these files than some of their predecessors, and Windows should sort things out when it is next booted.

There are several possible causes of Windows failing to shut down properly, but these days it is mainly associated with faulty driver software or other programs. Anyway, if this problem occurs before you start installing any of your own software, the problem is almost certainly due to drivers or other software supplied with the computer. Presumably other users of the same make and model of computer will be experiencing the same problem, and the manufacturer should quickly come up with a solution. The relevant customer support service should be able to supply you with details of this solution.

3

Customising
your laptop

Screen resolution

Having ascertained that your new laptop PC will boot into Windows properly and it can then be shut down without any problems, it is then ready for use. At least, in theory it is ready for use. In the real world it is usually necessary to do a certain amount of customising and install some

software before a new PC is ready to be used in earnest.

As supplied, the computer should have video settings that give good results with Windows itself, and with most application programs. The screen settings will usually have the monitor operating at its native resolution, which is the resolution that will give optimum results in most situations. However, under certain circumstances it can be advantageous to alter the video settings, including the resolution used.

Fig.3.1 *The Control Panel is accessed via the Start menu*

Fig.3.2 The Windows Vista Control Panel

For example, some games might not work very well with default settings. Changing to lower resolution and fewer colours will often give faster and smoother action, albeit with lower quality graphics. If your eyesight is less than perfect, using a lower screen resolution generally produces larger text and chunkier graphics that are easier to see. There are other occasions when a change in the video settings could be advantageous, such as when using the computer with an external monitor.

When you need to change the video settings, the first task is to launch the Windows Control Panel. The available routes to this built-in Windows program depend on how Windows is set up and the version you are using, but with a new installation of Vista there should be a menu entry for it in the right-hand column of the Start menu (Figure 3.1). In order to access the Control Panel it is then just a matter of left-clicking the Start button in the bottom left-hand corner of the Windows Desktop, and then left-clicking the Control Panel entry. A new window containing the Control Panel should then appear (Figure 3.2).

Next, left-click the Appearance and Personalization link in the left-hand section of the main panel. This will change the Control Panel to look like

Fig.3.3 Here the "Adjust screen resolution" link is activated

Figure 3.3. Here you must left-click the "Adjust screen resolution" link in the Personalization section, and this will launch a small window (Figure 3.4). The Screen Resolution slider control can be used to adjust the horizontal and vertical resolution of the screen, and there will typically be about half a dozen or more combinations on offer. However, there may be much less than this with a laptop computer, particularly if it has a small screen with a relatively low maximum resolution. Even so, there should still be the option of using two or three lower resolutions.

A computer's display is produced from thousands of tiny dots, or pixels as they are called. It is a sort of high-tech mosaic. Screen resolution is specified in terms of the number of pixels used. With a screen resolution of (say) 1024 by 768, there are 1024 pixels in each row, and 768 rows. This gives 786,432 pixels in total, which might sound a lot, but this is about the minimum that will give good results with much of the software in use today.

Opinions differ about the ideal screen resolution, but it is dependent on the type of software you will be running and the characteristics of the monitor you are using. In general, higher resolution is better, but only if your monitor can handle it properly. In the case of a laptop, its LCD

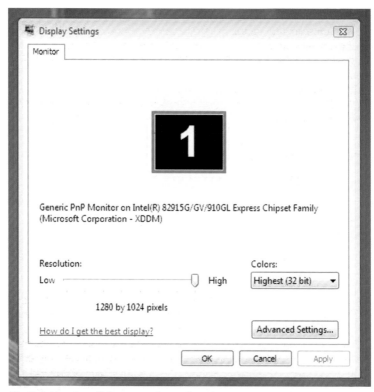

Fig.3.4 Use the slider control to adjust the screen resolution

screen should give good results at its highest resolution. However, and as already pointed out, your eyesight might not give optimum results with the screen used at its highest resolution setting. Using a PC is likely to be very tiring if you have to strain your eyesight in order to see the screen properly. It could be harmful to your eyesight as well. A laptop that has a small screen which normally runs at a high resolution might be easier to use if a lower resolution is selected. This is really a subjective matter, and you have to choose whatever resolution suits you best.

Colour depth

Colour depth is just a fancy term for the number of colours that can be displayed. This is a factor that is governed by the display adaptor in the

PC rather than the monitor, although with flat-panel screens the monitor might be the limiting factor. There is usually a choice of three colour depths on offer from the pop-down Colors menu in the bottom right-hand section of the Display Setting - Monitor window. These are 16, 24, and 32-bits, but there could be some lower options as well. With Vista and some display adaptors there could be a choice of one! This table shows the correlation between the number of bits and the number of colours provided:

Bits	Colours
4	16
8	256
16	65536
24	16.777 million
32	About 4,300 million

In general, higher colour depth settings give better looking results, especially when photographic images are displayed. On the other hand, the results obtained using 16-bit resolution are very good, and there is probably no point in going beyond 24-bit resolution. Bear in mind that greater colour depth tends to slow things down, and that some programs might not operate at a usable speed unless a fairly low colour depth is used. The optimum colour depth is the lowest one which gives a display quality that you find acceptable. There is no harm in trying various settings since it is easy to go back to the original one if the alternatives do not provide an improvement.

Having set the required screen resolution and colour depth, operate the Apply button. It is likely that Windows is overestimating the abilities of the monitor if the screen goes blank or produces an unstable image. The screen should return to normal in a few seconds though, because Windows will automatically return to the previous settings unless you tell it to keep the new ones. With the screen blank or in a mess it is not possible for you to do this, and obvious you would not do so anyway. A problem of this type is unlikely to occur when dealing with a laptop, but if it should happen it is probably best to simply abandon the idea of using the troublesome settings.

Deleting

As pointed out previously, it is likely that the new computer will have been supplied with some preinstalled software that is of no interest to you, and which might actually be a bit of a nuisance. Removing unwanted software from a PC is not usually too difficult, but it is important to go about things in the right fashion. Simply deleting the files and folders associated with programs you wish to remove is definitely going about things in the wrong fashion. It will certainly free some hard disc space, but deleting program files and folders is also likely to produce a few problems.

Most programs are installed onto the computer using an installation program, and this program does not simply make folders on the hard disc and copy files into them from the CD-ROM. It will also make changes to the Windows configuration files so that the program is properly integrated with the operating system. If you simply delete the program's directory structure to get rid of it, Windows will not be aware that the program has been removed. During the boot-up process the operating system will probably look for files associated with the deleted program, and will produce error messages when it fails to find them.

Matters are actually more involved than this, and there is another potential problem in that Windows utilizes shared files. This is where one file, such as a DLL type, is shared by two or more programs. In deleting a program and the other files in its directory structure you could also be deleting files needed by other programs. This could prevent other programs from working properly, or even from starting up at all.

If a program is loaded onto the hard disc using an installation program, the only safe way of removing it is to use an uninstaller program. There are three possible ways of handling this.

Custom uninstaller

Some programs load an uninstaller program onto the hard disc as part of the installation process. This program is then available via the Start menu if you choose All Programs, and then the folder with the name of the program concerned. If there is no folder icon for the program, just the normal entry that is used to launch it, then that program does not have an uninstaller or other additional software available. Even if there is a folder icon for the program, it is possible that there will be no uninstall option available there. The example of Figure 3.5 shows the submenu for the AVG Antivirus program, and this one does include an option to uninstall the program. Uninstaller programs are almost invariably automatic in operation, so you have to do little more than instruct a program of this type to go ahead with the removal of the program.

With any uninstaller software you may be asked if certain files should be removed. This mostly occurs where the program finds shared files that no longer appear to be shared. In days gone by it did not seem to matter whether you opted to

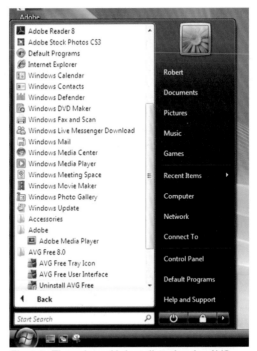

Fig.3.5 There is an Uninstall option for AVG program

remove or leave these files. Either way, Windows usually failed to work properly thereafter! These days things seem to be more reliable, and it is reasonably safe to accept either option. To leave the files in place is certainly the safest option, but it also results in files and possibly folders being left on the disc unnecessarily.

Windows uninstaller

Windows has a built-in uninstaller that can be accessed via the control panel. From the Start menu select Control Panel, and in the Control Panel (refer back to Figure 3.2) left-click the Uninstall a Program link in the Programs section. This takes you to the uninstaller section of the Control Panel, and the main section of the screen shows a list of the programs that can be uninstalled via this route (Figure 3.6). Removing a program is basically just a matter of selecting it from the list by left-clicking

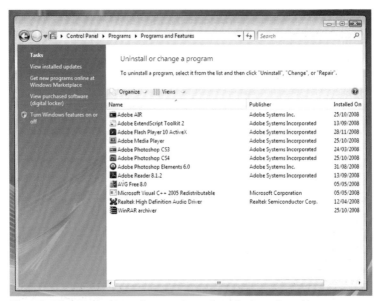

Fig.3.6 All the programs that can be uninstalled are listed here

its entry, and then operating the Uninstall/Change button. Changes to the system, including the removal of programs, will normally require you to confirm that you do actually wish to make the changes. This is a security measure designed to prevent hackers or rogue programs from making malicious alterations to the system. Operate the Continue button in order to carry on with the removal of the program.

The next step depends on the particular software that you are removing, and it may simply be necessary to confirm that you wish to remove the selected program. In many cases, and particularly in the case of major pieces of software, there will be more than one course of action open to you. In the example of Figure 3.7 there is a choice of installing or reinstalling the software, or removing it. In the current context, clearly it is the option of removing the program that is selected. The other option is used when it is necessary to install optional extras that were not chosen when the software was originally installed, or where a program has become corrupted and is not functioning correctly.

In theory, the list of removable programs should include all programs that have been added to the hard disc using an installation program. In

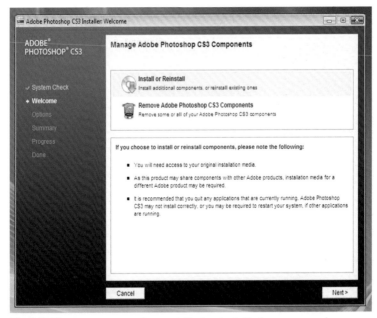

Fig.3.7 The program can be unstalled, reinstalled, or removed

practice there may be one or two that have not been installed "by the book" and can not be removed using this method. Some programs can only be removed using their own uninstaller program, while others have no means of removal at all. It is mainly older software that falls into the non-removable category, particularly programs that were written for Windows 3.1 and not one of the 32-bit versions of Windows. In fact it is very unusual for old Windows 3.1 software to have any means of removal. Fortunately, there is very little software of this vintage that is still in use.

These days it is more likely that there will be programs listed that you do not recognise. It is possible that one or more of these are pieces of malicious software that should be removed, but in most cases they are small programs that are installed with large programs. It seems to be increasingly common for substantial programs to be accompanied by one or more small utility programs that provide additional features. Software of this type should only be removed if you are sure that it does not provide a useful function.

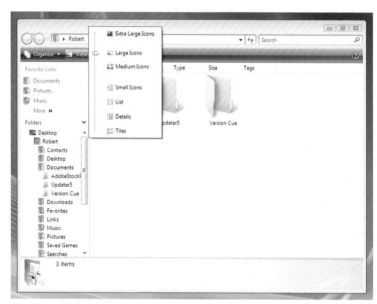

Fig.3.8 Set the slider control at the Details setting

Third party

There are uninstaller programs available that can be used to monitor an installation and then uninstall the software at some later time. As this feature is built into any modern version of Windows, and the vast majority of applications programs now either utilize the built-in facility or have their own uninstaller software, these programs are perhaps less useful than they once were.

Most will also assist in the removal of programs that they have not been used to install, and this is perhaps the more useful role. Most will also help with the removal of things like unwanted entries in the Start menu and act as general cleanup software, although Windows itself provides means of clearing some of this software debris.

Leftovers

Having removed a program by whatever means, you will sometimes find that there are still some files and folders associated with the program remaining on the hard disc. In some cases the remaining files are simply data or configuration files that have been generated while you were trying out or setting up the program. There should obviously be nothing of any importance here when deleting unused software from a new computer. Accordingly, there should be no problems if these files are deleted using Windows Explorer. In other cases the files could be system files that the uninstaller has decided not to remove in case they are needed by other applications. Removing files of this type is more risky and it is probably better to leave them in place.

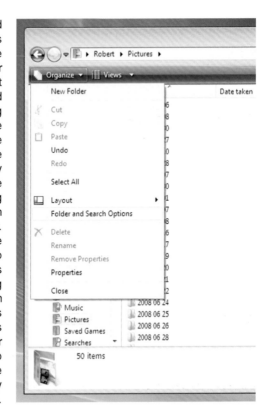

Fig.3.9 Select Folder and Search Options

Sometimes the folders may seem to be empty, but it is best to check carefully before removing them. An important point to bear in mind here is that not all files are shown when using the default settings of Windows Explorer. Using the default settings hidden files will live up to their name and files having certain extensions are not shown either. In normal use this can be helpful because it results in files that are likely to be of interest being shown, while those that are of no interest are hidden. This makes it much easier to find the files you require in a folder that contains large numbers of files.

It is clearly unhelpful when looking inside folders to see if they contain any files, as it could give the impression that a folder is empty when it

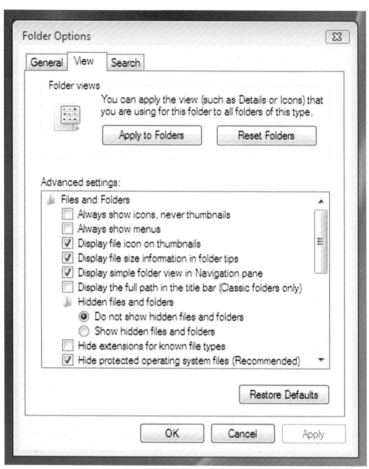

Fig.3.10 The options available under the View tab

does in fact contain files. Windows Explorer should be set to show as much detail about the files as possible. First go to the Views menu and select the Details option (Figure 3.8). This will result in the size, type, and date of each file being shown. Then go to the Organize menu, select Folder and Search Options (Figure 3.9), and then left-click on the View tab in the new Window that appears (Figure 3.10).

Under the Hidden Files entry in the main section of the window select the "Show hidden files and folders" option. The hidden files are certain critical system files, such as those associated with the Windows Registry, that are not normally displayed by Windows Explorer so that they can not be accidentally altered or erased by the user. I would recommend ticking the checkbox for "Display full path in title bar". This way you can always see exactly what folder you are investigating, even if it is one that is buried deep in a complex directory structure. However, with Windows Vista this only works if the Classic Folders option is selected in the General section of the Folder Options window. If it is selected, it is a good idea to deselect the "Hide extensions for known file types" option, so that the full filename is always shown.

Softly, softly

Unfortunately, it is not uncommon for uninstallers to leave large numbers of files on the hard disc. The uninstaller seems to go through its routine in standard fashion, and reports that the program has been fully removed, but an inspection of the hard disc reveals that a vast directory structure remains. I have encountered uninstallers that have left more than 50 megabytes of files on the disc, removing only about 10% of those initially installed.

Other uninstallers report that some files and folders could not be removed, and that they must be dealt with manually. Some uninstallers seem to concentrate on extricating the program from the operating system by removing references to the program in the Windows Registry, etc., rather than trying to remove all trace of it from the hard disc.

If you are simply trying to remove a troublesome program that produces annoying pop-up messages, uninstalling it should have the desired result and prevent the messages from appearing. If you are trying to free hard disc space, an uninstaller that leaves many megabytes of files in place is not very helpful. Try to keep things in perspective though. The hard disc drives used in laptop PCs generally have lower capacities than those used in desktop PCs, but the actual capacity is still likely to be quite high at around 80 gigabytes or more. Will removing (say) 100 megabytes (0.1 gigabytes) of files really make that much difference?

Removing leftover files is a bit risky, so due care needs to be taken if you do decide to go ahead. Most modern PCs are supplied with a disc that can be used to quickly restore the hard disc to its original state. Since no data will have been placed on the hard disc drive at this stage, there

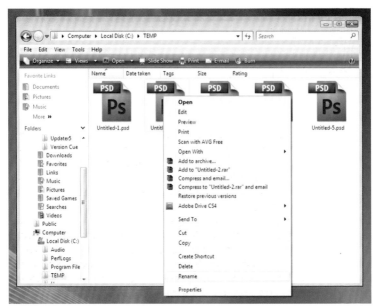

Fig.3.11 Select the Rename option from the pop-up menu

is not a lot to lose by taking things back to the beginning again. It is still better to avoid problems though, and take a softly, softly approach.

A safe way of handling things is to leave the directory structure and files intact, but change some file or folder names. If only a few files have been left behind, try adding a letter at the front of each filename. For example, a file called "drawprog.dll" could be renamed "zdrawprog.dll". This will prevent Windows from finding the file if it should be needed for some reason, but it is an easy matter for you to correct things by removing the "z" from the filename if problems occur.

If there are numerous files in a complex directory structure to deal with it is not practical to rename all the individual files. Instead, the name of the highest folder in the directory structure should be renamed. This should make it impossible for Windows to find the file unless it does a complete search of the hard disc, and the change is easily reversed if problems should occur. Provided the computer runs for a few days with no problems it should then be safe to go ahead and remove the files and folders.

A file or folder can be renamed by right-clicking its entry in Windows Explorer and selecting Rename from the pop-up menu (Figure 3.11). The name of the file or folder can then be edited in normal Windows fashion. Left-click any blank area of the Window once the necessary changes have been made.

User accounts

At least one user account is produced when Windows Vista is installed. There will often be two or three accounts, which are the Administrator account, a Guest account, and one for the user of the PC. The idea is for the Administrator account to be used by the person that looks after the computers in an office. The guest account is for use by someone who uses the computer only infrequently, and does not have an account of their own. Using the Guest account it is not possible to access the files of other users, and it is not possible to make changes such as installing or removing software. Apart from guests, each user of a PC has a separate account, with Windows set up the way that each user likes it when they use their account. As far as possible, each user effectively has their own PC, but obviously only one user at a time can login and utilise each PC.

Some computer retailers supply their PCs fully set up and ready for use, sometimes complete with several user accounts installed. However, things do not normally operate this way if you buy an "off the shelf" laptop PC, although it is often offered as a fairly pricey option. Any additional accounts you require normally have to be set up manually yourself.

Of course, user accounts can be irrelevant, especially in a home or small business environment. They may offer no advantages when there is only a single user for each PC. Even with two or three users per PC, they might prefer not to bother with the complication of separate accounts. On the other hand, some individual users do actually prefer to have several accounts, with Windows set up in a different fashion for each type of use. It is really a matter of personal preference.

Administrator

The Administrator account is usually reserved for making changes to the system or troubleshooting, since it gives full control over the system. As a minimum, there should be at least one additional account for normal

Fig.3.12 The Manage Accounts section of the Control Panel

use.   As pointed out previously, this will often be installed by default. However, it might be necessary to add this account yourself, and you will probably wish to add one or two extra accounts if the PC is for family use.

The first step in adding a new account is to go to the Control Panel and left-click the "Add or remove user accounts" link, which is in the User Accounts and Family Safety section.   This changes the window to something like the one shown in Figure 3.12. Left-click the link for "Create a new account", which switches the window to the one shown in Figure 3.13. The first task is to type a name for the account into the textbox. As with anything like this, try to use a meaningful name such as the nickname of the person who will use the account.

The two radio buttons are used to select the required type of account. An administrator account provides freedom to make changes to the system, but these abilities are not needed for day to day use of the computer. A standard account is generally considered to be the better choice for normal use, since the restrictions reduce the risk of the system being accidentally damaged. With a standard account it is still possible

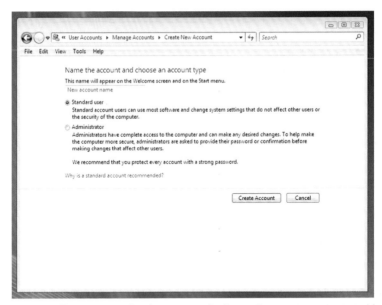

Fig.3.13 Enter a name for the account in the textbox

to make changes that will not affect the way in which others use the computer.

There are a few points to bear in mind if you opt for a standard account. You might not be able to install programs when using this type of account. Any that you do install might not be fully available to other users. Also, some programs produced prior to Windows 2000 and XP might not be usable with a limited account. As already pointed out, it is possible to make changes to the system that will only affect the standard account, but any wider-ranging changes, however trivial, are likely to be blocked. It might not be possible to undertake something as basic as uninstalling a program or deleting files when using this type of account. Consequently, there is no alternative to an administrator account if maximum flexibility is required.

Having selected the type of account using the radio buttons, operate the Create Account button. The original User Accounts window then returns, but it should now contain the newly created account (Figure 3.14). There are other facilities in the User Accounts window that enable the login and logoff settings to be altered. By default, the Welcome screen is

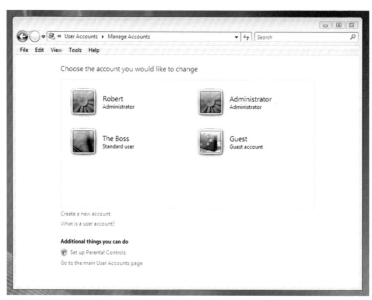

Fig.3.14 An entry has been added for the new account

Fig.3.15 Activate the Create Password link

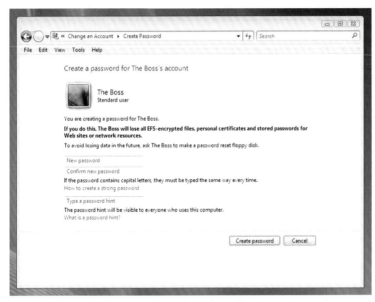

Fig.3.16 Enter the password into the two textboxes

shown at start-up, and you simply have to left-click the entry for the new account in order to use it. Note that the new account will start with a largely blank desktop. Each account has its own desktop and other settings, so each account can be customised with the best settings for its particular user.

Accounts are not password protected by default. To add a password, go to the User Accounts window and left-click the entry for the account that you wish to password protect. This switches the window to look like Figure 3.15, and here the Create Password link is activated. At the next window (Figure 3.16) the password is typed into the top two textboxes, and a hint is entered into the other textbox. The hint is something that will jog your memory if you should happen to forget the password. Next operate the Create Password button, which moves things on to the window of Figure 3.17, where the text beneath the account's icon should confirm that it is now password protected. This completes the process, and the password will be needed the next time you login to that account.

Fig.3.17 This windows confirms that the account is now password protected

Fig.3.18 The Classic version of the Windows Control Panel

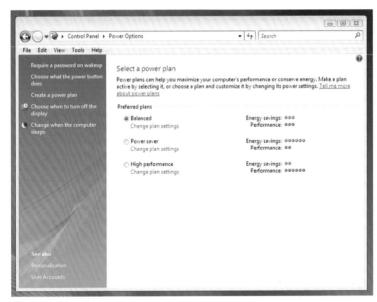

Fig.3.19 The Power Options window

On button

The button that is used to switch on the computer might have an additional function, or it might do nothing at all while the computer is switched on. The safe option is to have it do nothing at all, since there is a risk that it will be operated by mistake. This is the likely default setting, but it might have an alternative function. Windows enables the function of the On button to be altered by the user, but only a few options are available.

Start by going to the Control Panel, and then left-click the Switch to Classic View link near the top left-hand corner of the window. The Control Panel will then change to look something like Figure 3.18, but the exact icons present depends to some extent on the installed software and the computer's hardware configuration. However, there should always be a Power Options icon, and double-clicking it will produce the Power Options window (Figure 3.19).

The next step is to operate the "Choose what the power button does" link near the top left-hand corner of the window. The Power Options window then changes to look like Figure 3.20. It is the menu in the

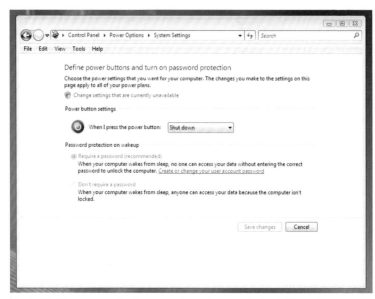

Fig.3.20 The Power Options window changes to look like this

middle of the window that is of interest here, and Figure 3.21 shows the options available for the power button menu.

Where available, the options available for the sleep button menu are exactly the same. Note though, that by no means all PCs, whether laptop or desktop, actually have a Sleep button. If there is one on your laptop it will probably have a crescent shaped icon that resembles a new moon. In the likely event that there is no Sleep button on your computer, there will probably be no settings for it in Windows. If there are options available for a nonexistent button, they will be of no practical importance.

These are the functions provided by each option for the power button:

Do Nothing

As it says, with this option selected the On button will be totally inoperative once the computer is running. While this limits the usefulness of the button, it does ensure that there is no danger of accidentally operating it and switching off the computer. Bear in mind that any accidental shutting down of the computer is not just a minor inconvenience. It is likely to result in a certain amount of work being lost, so it is best avoided!

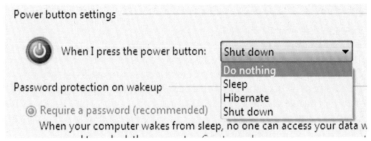

Fig.3.21 The options available for the Power button

Standby

If your PC has a Sleep button, then it is this option that the button will usually provide. In this context "sleep" and "standby" are alternative terms for the same thing. When a computer is set into the standby mode it might appear to be switched off, or there could still be a few obvious signs of activity. This depends on the particular computer concerned and the way in which it is set up. Typically, the monitor will switch off, as will the hard disc drive or drives.

The point of the Standby mode is to take the computer into a state where it consumes relatively little power. The main point of this when using a desktop PC is to save electricity and reduce the running costs. With a laptop it is more a matter of reducing the drain on the battery if the computer will not be used for a while, but you wish to avoid shutting it down and starting up again. You can place the computer into the Standby mode via the Start menu, so it is not essential to have a button set up to access this feature. On the other hand, having the On button or a Sleep button to access the standby mode is a convenient way of handling things.

When using the standby mode you should bear in mind that any work that has not been saved to the hard disc drive will not be saved automatically by the operating system when the computer enters the standby mode. Therefore, some work is likely to be lost if the power fails while the computer is in this mode. The risk is probably very small when using a desktop PC, but is clearly much higher when working with a laptop PC where the battery might be nearing exhaustion. When you use standby mode it is advisable to make sure that all work is saved to the hard disc first.

Hibernate

The hibernate mode is similar to the standby type, but it copies the contents of the computer's memory to the hard disc drive. This means that, in theory at any rate, it is possible for the system to switch off more of the hardware in this mode and it can recover from a power failure with all data intact. The price that is paid for this is that it takes much longer for the computer to enter this state and exit from it again. Also, the hibernate mode uses up hard disc space, so there must be enough free disc space for this mode work.

Although fine in theory, the hibernate mode does sometimes give problems in practice. Having entered this mode, you might find that the computer crashes or behaves erratically when you try to return it to normal operation. I would certainly recommend trying it a few times to check that it works reliably with your computer before making it a normal part of the way you work. This mode seems to be little used in practice.

Probably most PC users settle for the standby mode if they will not be using their laptop for relatively brief periods. In this mode it can be brought back to normal operation very quickly. If it will not be used for some time, probably the best approach is to make sure that everything is safely saved to disc and then shutdown the computer. Reboot the computer when you are ready to resume work. After all, the computer is in the ultimate power saving mode when it is switched off.

Shutdown

In this mode the computer shuts down when the button is operated, and there will probably be no pop-up window that gives you the option of changing your mind. Having pressed the button, the computer will immediately start its shut down routine. This has to be regarded as a bit risky, and this is probably not an option that is worth using. There will be other features available from the Power Options window, but initially anyway, the default settings should suffice.

Reset

It is normal for desktop PCs to have a reset switch that can be used to restart the computer if it hangs up so badly that there is no other way of restarting it. This switch is usually small and recessed into the case so that it is virtually impossible to operate it by accident. These days there are some desktop computers that do not have a reset switch, and it seems to be something of a rarity on laptop PCs.

With a desktop PC it is possible to reset the computer by switching it off, waiting a few seconds, and then turning it on again. This option is not a practical proposition with a laptop PC, since it is unlikely to have a conventional on/off switch. Even if a laptop PC is being run from its mains adaptor, "pulling the plug" on it will not necessarily switch it off. If there is a charged battery installed, it will continue to run for some time under battery power.

I suppose that as a last resort it would be possible to remove the battery for a few seconds, and then replace it. This is probably not a good idea though, and it is certainly not a course of action that I would recommend except as a last resort. If you delve into the computer's instruction manual you should find a means of switching it off if none of the usual routes is successful. Many laptops can be switched off by holding down the On switch for several seconds, but no doubt there are other methods in use.

Mouse

These days all laptop computers have a built-in pointing device of some kind, but many people still use a mouse when the computer is being used at home or in the office. Some even prefer to take a mouse when using a laptop on the move. The built-in pointing devices are ingenious and have improved over the years, but few users find them genuinely easy to use. My fingers are less agile than they used to be, and I find even the better ones virtually unusable. A mouse generally provides a much quicker and easier means of controlling the pointer.

The mouse is often problematic when first using a PC. Either the pointer goes flying across the screen with the slightest of mouse movements, or a huge amount of movement is needed in order to make it move a significant distance. The ideal mouse sensitivity is very much a matter of personal preference, and it also depends to some extent on the type of software in use. High sensitivity is suitable for most programs where the pointer will only be used to make menu selections. Low sensitivity is better in situations where very precise control of the pointer is needed, which mainly means graphics applications such as photo editing and technical drawing.

Windows enables the sensitivity of the mouse to be adjusted to suit each user's requirements. The first step is to go to the Windows Control Panel. If the Control Panel is not already in the Classic View, left-click the "Switch to Classic View" link, which is near the top left-hand corner of the window. There will be either a straightforward Mouse icon, or one that mentions a

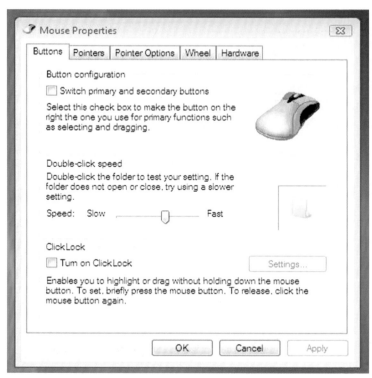

Fig.3.22 The Mouse Properties window

specific make and (or) model of mouse. This depends on whether the PC is equipped with a Microsoft mouse, a generic type, or one of the more upmarket mice. In this case the mouse is a Microsoft type and double-clicking the Mouse icon produces the standard version of the Mouse Properties window (Figure 3.22).

Click speed

The slider control near the middle of the window is very useful. It enables you to adjust the maximum time that can be used between the two mouse clicks of a double-click. It is likely that a slower double-click speed is required if you find that double-clicks tend to be ignored by Windows. If double-clicks are still ignored, either you are not releasing the button properly after the first mouse click, or the mouse is of low quality and it is

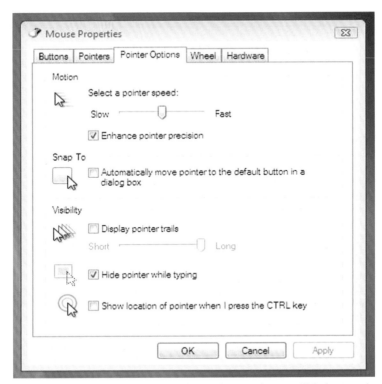

Fig.3.23 The upper slider control is used to set the sensitivity

not opening the switch contacts even though you are releasing the button sufficiently.

The control for the mouse sensitivity is obtained by left-clicking the Pointer Options tab near the top of the window. The Mouse Properties window then changes to look like Figure 3.23. The slider control near the top is the one that controls the sensitivity of the mouse, or the "mouse speed" in Microsoft's terminology.

If the control is moved to the right, a smaller amount of mouse movement will be needed in order to move the pointer a certain distance. Moving the slider to the left has the opposite effect, with greater mouse movement being needed in order to move the pointer a certain distance. Note that you can move the slider control by placing the pointer over it and then dragging it to a new position. Alternatively, left-clicking to one side of the control results in it moving one step in that direction.

Finding the optimum setting is really a matter of trial and error. You have to be practical about things, and using a low speed setting is not very practical if you have only a very limited amount of space for the mouse. The mouse keeps running over the edge of its allotted area, making it necessary to keep picking it up so it can be repositioned near the middle of its operating area. Lack of space is likely to be a common problem if you use a mouse with your laptop while working away from home or the office.

Windows provides a possible solution for those requiring precise control without having a large area for the mouse. In order to activate this facility it is merely necessary to tick the "Enhance pointer precision" checkbox. This is just below the speed control. The way this system works is very simple. When the pointer is moved quickly, the mouse has its normal degree of sensitivity. This is made quite high so that relatively little mouse movement is needed in order to move the pointer around the screen.

When the pointer is moved slowly, the sensitivity is automatically reduced so that precise positioning of the pointer is much easier. This system relies on the fact that users tend to go much more slowly and carefully when trying to position the pointer very accurately, and it can be very effective. Having two mouse sensitivities is sometimes called "mouse acceleration" incidentally. There will be other differences if you are using a mouse that has its own property window rather than the standard Windows type. Essentially the same controls are always present though, and it should not be too difficult to find the ones you need.

Built-in

Various types of built-in pointing device have been used over the years, but these days the vast majority of laptops use a small touchpad where the pointer is controlled by simply moving your finger over the pad (Figure 3.24). A variation on this scheme of things is essentially the same, but with a stylus being used instead of a finger, or there might be the option of using either. These touchpads seem to become ever more sophisticated, and they are more than basic pointing devices. Consequently, compared to an ordinary mouse they often have several more options available in the Mouse Properties window.

Some touchpads are pressure-sensitive, and a sensitivity setting for this facility. Pressure sensitivity is where the pressure on a touchpad or a graphics tablet is used to control some aspect of an application program. In paint and photo editing programs for instance, the pressure information is often used to control the width of lines produced with certain of the

Fig.3.24 The built-in pointing device of mopst laptops is a touchpad

program's drawing and painting tools. The pressure control determines the amount of force you need to use in order to utilize a facility of this type.

There might also be a setting that controls the way in which the system operates when your finger reaches an edge of the touchpad. By necessity, the touchpad has to be quite small. It is still possible to move the pointer from one side of the screen to the other, but only if a high pointer sped is set. The problem with this approach is that it makes precise control of the pointer very difficult. Moving your finger a few millimetres produces a large amount of onscreen movement by the pointer.

Setting a much lower pointer speed gives much more precise control, but you tend to run out of space on the touchpad when moving the pointer over a large distance. Of course, you merely have to remove your finger from the pad and reposition it somewhere near the opposite edge so that you can continue moving the pointer. This is a bit slow and cumbersome though.

There is sometimes a facility that results in the pointer continuing to move even though your finger has reached the edge of the touchpad and is stationary. This enables a relatively low pointer speed to be used, and accurate control to be obtained, but large movements of the pointer are still relatively easy. How well any clever features of this type work in practice is something that you have to determine for yourself. A feature that is a godsend for one user may well be completely unusable by another user.

The exact features available tend to vary slightly from one touchpad to another, so it is a matter of reading the instruction manual to determine what special facilities, if any, are available from your computer. The instruction manual should also include details of how to control them via the Windows Control Panel. If you will be using the touchpad a great deal, it makes sense to spend some time investigating its features, trying them for yourself, and "fine tuning" any that prove to be genuinely useful. A little time spent on this type of thing can make using a laptop computer much easier and more pleasant experience for the next few years.

Software manual

There are numerous references to instruction manuals in this book, but this all-important publication is something that will probably be conspicuously absent when you unpack your new laptop PC. It is likely that it will also be missing when you look down the checklist of items that should be included with the computer. The modern way of doing things is to have the instruction manual in software form, which usually means a PDF file. It will either be on a CD-ROM/DVD, or it will be preinstalled on the computer's hard disc.

There will be some printed instructions such as a Quick Start guide that will enable you to get the computer "up and running", but after that you have to refer to the software instruction manual. The printed documentation should include details of how to access the full manual. In many cases it is just a matter of selecting the appropriate option from the start menu, or double-clicking the manual's icon on the Windows desktop. Where the instruction manual is on a CD-ROM or DVD it is usually just a matter of inserting the disc into the computer's CD/DVD drive. The disc will then run automatically and the manual will appear on the screen.

The manual is often in the form of a file in PDF format, which is the one that is most commonly used for documentation stored on a disc. This format requires the Adobe Acrobat Reader program, which will almost certainly be supplied preinstalled on a modern laptop PC. It should certainly be preinstalled in cases where the computer has a manual that uses this format. This is a program that you will probably need sooner rather than later, so it is worth going to the Adobe web site (www.adobe.com) and downloading it if it is not already installed on your new laptop PC. There is no charge for downloading, using, and installing this program. It has no restrictions, but it is only a file reader, so it is not possible to use it for editing PDF files. On the other hand, you can print out individual pages, page ranges, or the whole manual.

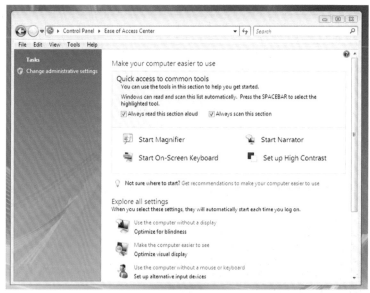

Fig.3.25 The main window for the Ease of Access Center

Ease of Access Center

Windows has some built-in facilities that are intended to make the computer easier to use, particularly for those of us with eyesight that is less than perfect. These facilities can be accessed via the Ease of Access Center, which is available by going to the Classic version of the Control Panel and double-clicking the Ease of Access Center's icon. This changes the Control Panel to the one shown in Figure 3.25.

It is worth trying the Magnifier program, which provides a magnified view of the area around the pointer or cursor. In addition to the window that shows the magnified view, a small control panel is launched when the Magnifier program is run. This enables various aspects of the magnified view to be controlled, such as the degree of magnification, and the position of the magnified view on the screen. This facility is included primarily as a means of reading small text more easily, but it will magnify any area of the screen, whether it contains text or graphics (Figure 3.26). The Magnifier program seems to work better with some computers than it does with others, and the pointer can become a bit flashy and intermittent when this program is running. It is certainly worth trying

Fig.3.26 The Magnifier works with grapics as well as areas of text

though, and there are more sophisticated commercial magnifier programs available if you need something better.

Taking things a stage further, you can try the Narrator program. This can be set up in various ways, but its basic action is to describe the buttons, etc., in the current window, and to read text. It can also tell you which keys you are operating when using the keyboard. The ability of the program to read blocks of text is probably the one that is of most general use. Rather than straining your eyes or using the Magnifier program to make reading text easier, you simply have the Narrator program read it to you via the computer's audio system. It does not work with most text on web pages, but it is possible to use the Windows Copy and Paste facilities to transfer the text word processor. The built-in Wordpad program of Windows (Start – All Programs – Accessories – Wordpad) is more than adequate for this purpose. In the browser, drag the pointer through the text you wish to have read and then select Copy from the Edit menu. Then go to the word processor and select Paste from the Edit menu. If the Narrator program is running, it should then read the text, albeit with an American accent.

Internet and security

Be prepared

Computer security has become an increasingly important matter over the years. It was originally something of little importance to most computer users, since computer viruses and other malicious programs were only spread via infected discs. There was little swapping of discs, and not all discs were potential carriers of a computer infection. While most users could not totally discount the risk of a computer infection, it took no more than a few simple precautions to render the risk insignificant.

Things changed when the Internet came into being and its popularity spread. If someone tried to invent a system that would make it easy for an infection to be rapidly spread to a large number of computers, it would probably be remarkably similar to the Internet. The nature of the threat also changed when the Internet and Internet commerce became popular. The original computer viruses either did very little at all to the infected computer, or tried to render it unusable. The current threats tend to be more sinister, and are mostly designed to steal passwords and other personal information, or to enable the infected computer to be taken over for use in illegal activities.

Despite the very real risks, many computer users still take the view that they do not need antivirus software until and unless a virus actually attacks their PC. This is a rather short-sighted attitude and one that is asking for trouble. By the time that you know a virus has infected your PC it is likely that a substantial amount of damage will have already been done to the system files and (or) your own data files. Using antivirus software to help sort out the mess after a virus has struck is "shutting the stable door after the horse has bolted". The virus may indeed be removed by the antivirus software, but there may be no way of correcting all the damage that has been done.

Another point to bear in mind is that your PC could be rendered unbootable by the virus. Many viruses attack the operating system and will try to make the system unbootable. Most antivirus programs do some basic checks as part of the installation process. The program will not be installed if any hint of a virus is detected. The reason for this is that the installation process involves copying numerous files onto the hard disc and making changes to some of the Windows system files. This can provide an opportunity for the virus to spread and do further damage.

Many antivirus programs can be used once a virus has attacked a PC, and even if the PC can not be booted into Windows. The usual approach is to have some form of emergency boot disc. If the PC becomes unbootable and a virus is thought to be the cause, the PC is booted from the boot disc. A series of checks are then performed, with the other discs being used as and when required. The drawback of this method is that the emergency disc will be something less than fully up-to-date, and may not be able to handle some of the more recent viruses.

Virus?

The non-technical press tend to call any form of software that attacks computers a virus. A virus is a specific type of program though, and represents just one of several types that can attack a computer. Initially, someone attaches the virus to a piece of software, and then finds a way of getting that software into computer systems. These days the Internet is the most likely route for the infection to be spread, but it is important not to overlook the fact that there are other means of propagating viruses, such as discs and Flash memory cards.

Anyway, having introduced a virus into a system via one route or another, it will attack that system and try to replicate itself. Some viruses only attack the boot sector of a system disc. This is the part of the disc that the computer uses to boot into the operating system. Other viruses will try to attach themselves to any file of the appropriate type, which usually means a program file of some sort. The attraction of a program file is that the user will probably run the program before too long, which gives the virus a chance to spread the infection and (or) or start attacking the computer system.

At one time there were only two possible ways in which a virus could attack a computer. One way was for the virus to attach itself to a program file that the user then ran on his or her computer. The other was for someone to leave an infected floppy disc in the computer when it was switched off. On switching the computer on again the floppy disc was used as the boot disc, activating the virus in the disc's boot sector.

Script virus

These days you have to be suspicious of many more types of file. Many applications programs such as word processors and spreadsheets have the ability to automate tasks using scripts or macros as they are also known. The application effectively has a built-in programming language and the script or macro is a form of program. This makes it possible for viruses or other harmful programs to be present in many types of data file. Scripts are also used in some web pages, and viruses can be hidden in these JavaScript programs, Java applets, etc. There are other potential sources of infection such as Email attachments.

I would not wish to give the impression that all files, web pages, and Emails are potential sources of script or macro viruses. There are some types of file where there is no obvious way for them to carry a virus or other harmful program. Nevertheless, it is probably best to regard all files and Emails with a degree of suspicion. As explained later in this chapter, even though simple text can not carry a true virus, it can carry a virus of sorts.

Benign virus

It tends to be assumed that all viruses try to harm the infected computer system, but many viruses actually do very little. Some viruses do nothing more than display a daft message on the screen when a certain date is reached, or on a particular date each year. Viruses such as this certainly have a degree of nuisance value, but they are not harmful. I would not wish to give the impression that most viruses are harmless. Many computer viruses do indeed try to do serious damage to the infected system. If in doubt you have to assume that a virus is harmful.

Worm

A worm is a program that replicates itself, usually from one disc to another, or from one system to another via a local network or the Internet. Like a virus, a worm is not necessarily harmful. In recent times many of the worldwide virus scares have actually been caused by worms transmitted via Email, and not by what would normally be accepted as a virus.

The usual ploy is for the worm to send a copy of itself to every address in the Email address book of the infected system. A worm spread in this way, even if it is not intrinsically harmful, can have serious consequences. There can be a sudden upsurge in the amount of Email traffic, possibly causing parts of the Email system to seriously slow down or even crash. Some worms compromise the security of the infected system, perhaps enabling it to be used by a hacker for sending spam for example.

Trojan horse

A Trojan horse, or just plain Trojan as it is now often called, is a program that is supposed to be one thing but is actually another. In the early days many Trojans were in the form of free software, and in particular, free antivirus programs. The users obtained nasty shocks when the programs were run, with their computer systems being attacked. Like viruses, some Trojans do nothing more than display stupid messages, but others attack the disc files, damage the boot sector of the hard disc, and so on.

A backdoor Trojan is the same as the standard variety in that it is supplied in the form of a program that is supposed to be one thing but is actually another. In some cases nothing appears to happen when you install the program. In other cases the program might actually install and run as expected. In both cases one or two small programs will have been installed on the computer and set to run when the computer is booted.

One ploy is to have programs that produce log files showing which programs you have run and Internet sites that you have visited. The log will usually include any key presses as well. The idea is for the log file to provide passwords to things such as your Email account, online bank account, and so on. Someone hacking into your computer system will usually look for the log files, and could obviously gain access to important information from these files. Another ploy is to have a program that makes it easier for hackers to break into your computer system. A backdoor Trojan does not attack the infected computer in the same way as some viruses, and it does not try to spread the infection to other discs or computers, but it is potentially more serious than a virus.

Spyware/Adware

Spyware programs monitor system activity and send information to another computer by way of the Internet. There are really two types of spyware, and one tries to obtain passwords and send them to another computer. This takes things a step further than the backdoor Trojan programs mentioned earlier. Spyware is usually hidden in other software in Trojan fashion.

The second type of spyware is more correctly called adware. In common with spyware, it gathers information and sends it to another computer via the Internet. Adware is not designed to steal passwords or other security information from your PC. Its purpose is usually to gather information for marketing purposes, and this typically means gathering and sending details of the web sites you have visited. Some free programs are supported by banner advertising, and the adware is used to select advertisements that are likely to be of interest to you.

Programs that are supported by adware have not always made this fact clear during the installation process. Sometimes the use of adware was pointed out in the End User License Agreement, but probably few people bother to read the "fine print". These days the more respectable software companies that use this method of raising advertising revenues make it clear that the adware will be installed together with the main program. There is often the option of buying a "clean" copy of the program. Others try to con you into installing the adware by using the normal tricks.

Provided you know that it is being installed and are happy to have it on your PC, adware is not a major security risk. It is sending information about your surfing habits, but you have given permission for it to do so. If you feel that this is an invasion of privacy, then do not consent to it being installed. The situation is different if you are tricked into installing adware. Then it does clearly become an invasion of your privacy and you should remove any software of this type from your PC. Note that if you consent to adware being installed on your PC and then change your mind, removing it will probably result in the free software it supports being disabled or uninstalled.

Dialers

A dialer is a program that uses a modem and an ordinary dial-up connection to connect your PC to another computer system. Dialers probably have numerous legitimate applications, but they are mainly associated with various types of scam. An early one was a promise of free pornographic material that required a special program to be downloaded. This program was, of course, the dialer, which proceeded to call a high cost number in a country thousands of miles away. In due course the user received an astronomic telephone bill.

A modern variation on this is where users are tricked into downloading a dialer, often with the promise of free software of some description. User goes onto the Internet in the usual way via their dial-up connections, and everything might appear to be perfectly normal. What is actually happening though is that they are not connecting to the Internet via their normal Internet service provider (ISP). Instead, the dialer is connecting them to a different ISP that is probably thousands of miles away and is costing a fortune in telephone charges. Again, the problem is very apparent when the telephone bill arrives.

Dialers are not usually a problem for broadband users. There is no way a dialer can connect your PC to the Internet or another computer system via a non-existent dial-up connection. There is a slight risk if your PC is equipped with a telephone modem for sending and receiving faxes. The risk is relatively small though, since you would presumably notice that the modem was being used for no apparent reason.

Hoax virus

A hoax virus might sound innocuous enough and just a bit of a joke, but it has the potential to spread across the world causing damage to computer systems. The hoax is usually received in the form of an Email from someone that has contacted you previously. They say that the Email they sent you previously was infected with a virus, and the Email then goes on to provide information on how to remove the virus. This usually entails searching for one or more files on your PC's hard disc drive and erasing them.

Of course, there was no virus in the initial Email. The person that sent the initial Email could be the hoaxer, or they might have been fooled by the hoax themselves. The hoax Email suggests that you contact everyone that you have emailed recently, telling them that their computer could be infected and giving them the instructions for the "cure". This is the main way in which a hoax virus is propagated. The files that you are instructed to remove could be of no real consequence, or they could be important system files. It is best not to fall for the hoax and find out which.

These hoax viruses demonstrate the point that all the antivirus software in the world will not provide full protection for your PC. They are simple text files that do not do any direct harm to your PC, and can not be kept at bay by software. Ultimately it is up to you to use some common sense and provide the final line of defence. A quick check on the Internet will usually provide details of hoax viruses and prevent you from doing anything silly.

Phishing

Note that there are other scams that involve hoax emails. Recently there have been numerous instances of "phishing" attacks, where Emails are sent to customers of online financial companies. These Emails purport to come from the company concerned, and they ask customers to provide their passwords and other account details. This is usually done by trying to get the customer to log onto a dummy version of the bank's Internet site. The dummy site is accessed via a link in the Email, and the site normally looks largely authentic, and is likely to be a clone of the genuine article.

It is not the real thing though, and anyone falling for it has their account details stolen. There is usually a good indication that the site is not the real thing if you look at the site address displayed by the browser. This will almost certainly be incorrect if the site is not the one it purports to be. These days the main browser programs have a facility that spots most fraudulent sites and warns you not to enter them. It is advisable to opt for this phishing filter facility. However, the best way to avoid phishing scams is to always log into financial sites in the normal way, and not via a link provided in an Email, or anywhere else.

Supplied software

The importance of antivirus software is such that many PCs are now supplied with an antivirus program as part of the preinstalled bundle of software. Unfortunately, although the antivirus software is fully functioning, it normally comes with quite a short subscription to the manufacturers update service. There is not usually any limit to the length of time that the software can be used, but the virus definition database starts to become out of date once the update subscription has expired. This means that the program will be very good at finding old viruses, but its ability to detect new ones soon becomes non-existent.

There is no problem here if you are satisfied with the program and you are prepared to pay the subscription charge for the update service. It is important to realise that the degree of protection offered by the program will effectively diminish with the passage of time if you continue to use it without bothering with updates. The program will still provide some protection, but it will also start to leave your computer open to attack by an ever increasing range of viruses and other malicious software. An attack is more likely to involve a recent virus than an ancient one, so the computer is left vulnerable to the most likely threats.

Free protection

There are better ways of handling things than continuing to use a commercial antivirus program that is relying on out of date virus definitions. Windows Vista does actually have a built-in program that is designed to protect the computer from various types of threat, and this is called Windows Defender. This is normally included as part of a standard Windows Vista installation, so it will almost certainly run automatically each time your laptop is switched on.

Windows Defender runs in the background, protecting your computer all the time it is switched on. The main program can be accessed by going to the Start menu, selecting All Programs, and then choosing Windows Defender from the menu. This produces a window like the

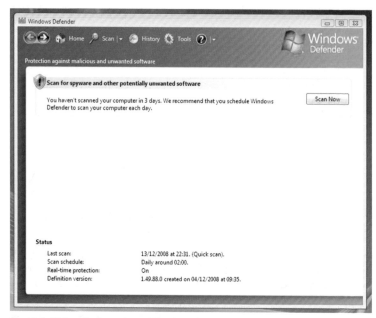

Fig.4.1 This window shows the last time a scan was performed

one shown in Figure 4.1, and this provides information about the last time that Windows Defender did a scan of the system. A scan can be started manually by operating the Scan Now button, and in due course this will provide the scan results. No threats were found in the example of Figure 4.2, and therefore none were removed from the system.

It is possible to control the way in which Windows Defender operates by first left-clicking the Tools icon near the top of the window, which changes

Fig.4.2 This scan found no threats present

it to look like Figure 4.3. Next operate the Options button, and the window will then change to the one shown in Figure 4.4. There are various parameters that can be altered here, but in most cases the default settings will suffice. However, you might like to alter the time at which automatic scanning takes place. The default is usually for

Fig.4.3 The Tools and Settings section of Windows Defender

this to occur at about 2:00 in the morning, when it is unlikely that your laptop will be running. A more suitable time can then be selected from the pop-down menu.

As with most software of this general type, the program can undertake a quick scan or a more thorough type. Obviously a thorough scan is preferable, but each scan of this type can take a very long time. In fact with many PCs it takes too long to be practical for daily scanning. Quick scanning is then the more practical choice, perhaps with the occasional full scan started manually. Of course, it is not necessary to have a daily scan at all, and one of the menus offers scans at other intervals. The scanning can be switched off completely by removing the tick in the "Automatically scan my computer" checkbox.

Fig.4.4 The scan time, type, and frequency can be set here

Other programs

Windows Defender is primarily designed to counter spyware and pop-up advertisements on web pages, and it is not intended to be a complete solution to problems with malicious software. It should be used in addition to antivirus software rather than instead of it. If you do not wish to pay for a subscription to commercial antivirus software there are some good free alternatives available.

One option is to use a free online virus checking facility to periodically scan your PC, but the drawback of this method is that there is no real-time protection for your PC. By the time you do a virus scan it is possible that a virus could have been spreading across your files for some time. By the time it is detected and removed it is likely that a significant amount of damage would already have been done.

An antivirus program running on your PC will, like Windows Defender, provide real-time protection. In other words, it monitors disc drive activity, Internet activity, or anything that might involve a virus or other malicious program. If any suspicious files are detected, there is an attempt to alter system files, or any dubious activity is detected, the user is warned. In most cases the virus or other malicious program is blocked or removed from the system before it has a chance to do any harm.

The alternative to using online virus scanning is to download and install a free antivirus program. There are one or two totally free antivirus programs available on the Internet, where you do not even have to pay for any online updates to the database. The free version of AVG 8.0 from Grisoft is one that is certainly worth trying. The Grisoft site is at:

www.grisoft.com

On the home page there might be a link to the free version of the program, but it does not seem to

Fig.4.5 The AVG Free homepage

feature quite as prominently in the home page as it did in the past. At the time of writing this, the web address for Grisoft's free software is:

http://free.avg.com/download-avg-anti-virus-free-edition

Having found the right page, using a search engine if necessary, it will look something like the web page of Figure 4.5. This gives some information about the free software available from Grisoft, including their antivirus program. You will probably have to go through two or three pages before you reach the link that enables the program file to be downloaded. Make sure you choose the download link for the correct operating system, which will presumably be the one for Windows. It is actually just a single file that is downloaded, but this is an archive that contains all the installation files. You can download the file to the hard disc and then run it, but there will usually be an option to download and automatically run the file. This is the easier way of doing things. There is an instruction manual for the program in PDF format, which can be read online or downloaded to your PC. Installation of AVG Free is fairly straightforward and follows along the normal lines for Windows software.

Daily updates to AVG are available free of charge, so it should always be reasonably up-to-date. This program has a reputation for being very efficient, and it did once detect a couple of backdoor Trojan programs on my system that a certain well known commercial program had failed to detect. It is certainly one of the best freebies on the Internet, and it generally performs very well in comparison to commercial equivalents.

AVG has a useful range of facilities and it is a very capable program. Like Windows Defender, it runs in the background and provides real-time protection, but you can also go into the main program. It can be launched via the normal routes, and by default there will be a quick-launch button near the bottom left-hand corner of the Windows Desktop. The program has various sections, and the initial window provides access to them (Figure 4.6). There is a facility here that manually updates the program's virus database, but the program will automatically update provided an active Internet link is available when the program is booted into Windows.

In common with most antivirus programs you can set it to scan the system on a regular basis (Figure 4.7). This section of the program is accessed by first selecting Advanced Settings from the Tools menu. Then left-click Schedules and Scheduled Scans in the directory tree in the left-hand column of the new window that appears.

Manual scanning is also available, and this is another standard feature for this type of software. Scanning of the entire computer or a selected

part can be initiated via the Computer Scanner tab of the main program window (Figure 4.8). Normally a complete scan of the entire system is used, but it can sometimes be useful to scan (say) a removeable disc or a particular folder.

Fig.4.6 This window provides access to the various sections of the program

The window changes to look something like Figure 4.9 if you opt for selected scanning.

The main panel shows a directory tree containing an entry for each section of the computer that can be scanned. Each section has a checkbox, and ticking a box selects that part of the computer for scanning. Where appropriate, left-clicking the "+" marking next to an entry will expand

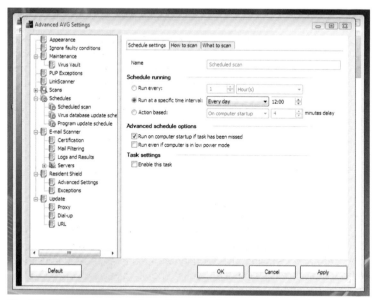

Fig.4.7 The program can be set to scan the system regularly

that entry to show its subfolders. This makes it possible to scan specific folders or subfolders rather than an entire disc.

The test results will show what action was taken if one or more viruses were detected. The action taken depends on how the program is set up and precisely what it finds. It will leave the infected file

Fig.4.8 The whole computer or specific parts can be scanned

unchanged, delete it, or quarantine the file by moving to the secure folder that is called the "Virus Vault" in AVG terminology. Alternatively, it will do nothing and ask the user to select the required option.

Automatic updates

Hackers try to exploit weaknesses in Windows, browsers, and other software that make the programs vulnerable to attack. The software writers are continually finding ways of making their programs more resilient against attacks, and soon find ways of fixing any flaws in their programs. This results in frequent updates being made available for Windows, and slightly less frequently for many other programs. Some updates are not security related, and installing them is not crucial. This is not to say that they are not worthwhile, as the changes to the program will usually fix minor problems, add new features, or improve existing ones. However, failing to install them will not leave your computer at risk.

The same is not true of security updates, and it is important to have these installed at the earliest possible opportunity. Without them your computer is left at risk of attack, and it will be especially vulnerable if you use some form of broadband Internet connection. Keeping Windows up-to-date and installing any security updates is especially important. Without them it is possible that hackers could take over your PC, steal sensitive information stored on it, or use it for illegal attacks on other computers. For the same reason it is also important to keep your web browser up-to-date.

Windows Vista has a built-in update facility that is accessed by going to the Classic version of the Control Panel and double-clicking the Windows Update icon. This launches the window shown in Figure 4.10, and the upper section of the main panel provides details of any updates that are available. The control button gives the option of actually installing them, should you wish to do so.

Fig.4.9 Use this window to select the parts of the computer that will be scanned

An alternative way of tackling Windows updates is to opt for them to be installed automatically. This method of updating might have been set up when Windows was installed, but if not it can be selected by operating

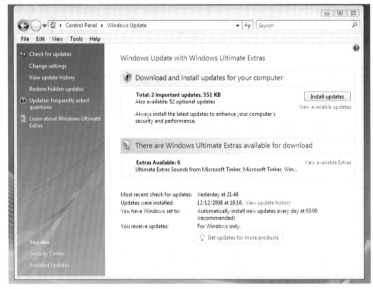

Fig.4.10 This window gives details of the available Windows updates

the Change Settings link in the left-hand section of the Control Panel. It then changes to look like Figure 4.11, where there are various update options available. The simplest approach is to have all updates installed automatically, and this is a good way of doing things if the computer is normally

Fig.4.11 Various update options are available

connected to a fast broadband connection. This method is probably not a practical proposition if a slower Internet connection is used, such as a dial-up type, or it is only used occasionally with a fast connection.

A more selective approach is then a better way of going about things, as it is then possible to opt out of any large downloads that will be of little or no benefit to you. The option to select is the one that lets you choose the updates and then downloads only those that have been selected. The other option downloads all updates and then lets you choose the ones you wish to actually install. This method does not reduce the amount of update data that is downloaded, but could still have the slight advantage of preventing hard disc space being consumed by unnecessary updates.

Firewall

Further protection from attack can be provided by using a firewall program. A firewall is used to block access to your PC, and in most cases it is access to your PC via the Internet that is blocked. Of course, a firewall is of no practical value if it blocks communication from one PC to another and access via the Internet. What it is actually doing is preventing unauthorised access to the protected PC. When you access an Internet site your PC sends messages to the server hosting that site, and these messages request the pages you wish to view. Having requested information, the PC expects information to be sent from the appropriate server, and it accepts that information when it is received. A firewall does not interfere with this type of Internet activity provided it is set up correctly.

It is a different matter when another system tries to access your PC when you have not instigated the initial contact. The firewall will treat this attempted entry as an attack and will block it. Of course, the attempt at accessing your PC might not be an attack, and a firewall can result in legitimate access being blocked. Something like peer-to-peer file swapping is likely to fail or operate in a limited fashion. The sharing of files and resources on a local area network could also be blocked. A practical firewall enables the user to permit certain types of access so that the computer can work normally while most unauthorised access is still blocked. However, doing so does reduce the degree of protection provided by the firewall.

Windows Firewall

There is a firewall program built into Windows XP and Vista. Unless you use the original version of Windows XP with no major updates included, the firewall will be activated by default. It is easy to check whether the firewall program is switched on, and it is just a matter of going to the Classic version of the Windows Control Panel and double-clicking the Windows Firewall icon. This changes the Control Panel to look like Figure 4.12, and in this example the Firewall is indeed switched on. If it is switched off, activating the "Turn Windows Firewall on or off" link alters the Control Panel so that it provides an option to switch it on.

The current Windows Firewall is better than the original version, but it is still fairly basic and not the equal of most third-party firewall programs. Consequently, if you have an alternative firewall program, in most cases it will be best if this is used and the built-in program is switched off. The built-in firewall will probably not offer any facility that is not available from the third-party alternative.

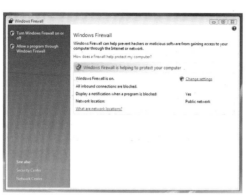

Fig.4.12 On this system the Windows Firewall program is switched on

Keep it safe

It is easy to fall into the trap of putting plenty of time and effort into keeping your data safe from Internet attacks, while ignoring the fact that the computer itself is vulnerable to being physically stolen. In recent times there has been a string of news stories about laptop computers that have been stolen, together with the masses of personal data stored on their hard disc drives. Laptop PCs are probably the favourite target of opportunist thieves. If you leave a laptop unattended and somewhere other than at home it is quite likely to be stolen before too long. In fact it is quite likely to be stolen even if you only leave it semi unattended. When out and about with a laptop PC it should not be let out of your sight, and it should preferably not go out of your grasp.

Ideally you should not store any personal data on a laptop PC. Sensitive data should be stored on discs or Flash memory cards and left at home, safely stored out of sight where a burglar will not easily find them. If this is not a practical proposition, files containing sensitive data should be encrypted and password protected. There are commercial programs that provide this function. Also, the popular compression and archiving programs such as WinZip and WinRar can encrypt and password protect files that have been compressed singly, or compressed as a group and stored together in a single archive file.

Windows and some software will often offer a facility to remember usernames and sometimes passwords as well. Using facilities such as these makes it easier to use Email accounts, etc., but it also means that anyone who gains possession of your computer has equally easy access to them. It is advisable not to use anything of this type with a laptop PC, and to always settle for the slow but safe alternative of entering usernames and passwords manually.

Getting connected

In order to put your computer at risk of an attack via the Internet you must first get it connected to the worldwide web. Getting any computer connected to the Internet used to be something of an ordeal, but unless you are very unlucky, these days it is reasonably straightforward. There is insufficient space available here to describe in detail the various ways of getting a laptop connected to the Internet, but the following sections cover the basics of the main methods. There are four normal ways of getting a laptop PC connected to the Internet:

Dial-up

With a dial-up connection you simply connect the modem output of the laptop to an ordinary telephone socket, and a suitable connecting lead is often supplied with the computer. If not, it is a standard lead that can be obtained from any computer store. Your Internet service provider (ISP) should provide detailed information about getting started, and they often supply a disc that makes any necessary adjustments to the setup of your computer.

This is likely to be the cheapest and easiest way of obtaining an Internet connection, but bear in mind that the speed of a dial-up connection is very slow in comparison to any form of broadband connection. A typical broadband connection is something like a hundred times faster than a good dial-up type. A dial-up connection is all right for surfing the Internet, but it is not suitable for much beyond that. Another point to keep in mind is that many dial-up services are only available from your home telephone number, and can not be used with any telephone connection that happens to be available when you are on the move. Last, and by no means least, the telephone line can not be used for other purposes while the dial-up connection is active. The other methods of Internet connection leave your telephone line free for normal use.

Wired broadband

Actually there are two different types of wired broadband connection, and one of these uses an ordinary telephone line plus some additional equipment connected to your telephone line at the exchange, plus some equipment to connect your computer to the telephone line. This is an ADSL (Asymmetric Digital Subscriber Line) Internet connection, and it is the most popular type. There is usually a charge for setting up an ADSL broadband connection, although this is often waived if you sign up to the service for a minimum period that is typically one or two years.

A special modem is needed for an ADSL Internet link, and the modem socket of a laptop is of no use for this type of connection. An ADSL modem usually connects to the computer via a USB port or the Ethernet networking port. Some ADSL modems have provision for either method. Modern ADSL connections are very fast, but bear in mind that the quoted speeds are usually the theoretical maximums and not a guaranteed minimum. In general, ADSL connections are fast if you live near to the telephone exchange, and relatively slow if you are situated a longer distance from it. ADSL broadband might not be available if you live too far from the telephone exchange.

The alternative type of wired broadband connection is not strictly speaking a wired type, since the signals are carried via fibre-optic cables rather than conventional wires. This method has the advantage of always working at full speed, with no dependence on the telephone exchange

Fig.4.13 The rear panel of a wi-fi router and broadband modem

being a reasonably short distance away. This is due to the use of fibre-optic cables that are entirely separate from the normal telephone system. The main drawback is that this method is only available if your street has been "wired" with the fibre-optic cables.

Wireless broadband

A wireless broadband (wi-fi) connection is usually in the form of an add-on system for a wired broadband connection. Instead of a broadband modem, a combined modem and wi-fi router is used (Figure 4.13). There are sockets on this device that enable it to connect to the telephone socket and several computers via their Ethernet networking ports. There is also an aerial, or perhaps two aerials, that enable the router to connect wirelessly to computers that are equipped with a suitable wi-fi adaptor. These days an adaptor of this type is a standard feature of most laptop PCs.

The router enables several computers to share a single broadband Internet connection, with each user being able to independently access the Internet. It also enables data to be shared between any computers connected to the network. However, the network does not have to consist of the modem/router and half a dozen or more computers. It can simply comprise the modem/router and a laptop PC.

Using a wireless connection is more complicated and expensive than using a wired connection to a broadband modem, but it does have its advantages. The main one is that it is possible to use the Internet connection with the computer anywhere within a radius of about 50 metres from the modem/router. If you wish to use the Internet connection with the laptop in the garden, next-door, or an outhouse, there should be no difficulty in doing so. Just set up the laptop in the normal way and start surfing.

It is often possible to access the Internet while on the move using what are called "wireless hotspots". These offer Internet access in numerous locations around the world, with many town and cities in the UK now having large numbers of these hotspots. A wireless hotspot is a wireless access point that connects to some form of Internet service. This will typically be a high-speed ADSL broadband connection, but it could be some other type of broadband service. It should certainly be something much faster than an ordinary dialup connection, but bear in mind that you might have to share the service with other users, which could noticeably slow things down.

The idea is to have hotspots in restaurants, cafes, motorway service stations, hotels, trains, airports, or anywhere convenient for potential users. As one would expect, these services are not usually free, and the hourly connection rates are quite high. Even so, this method can be cost-effective for those requiring Internet access on the move. Some hotspots are provided free of charge, so you might get lucky from time to time and obtain free Internet access.

USB dongle

A USB dongle is a small gadget that is plugged into a USB port of your computer, and it is then possible to access the Internet via a mobile telephone network. This approach to things is not exactly new, but it has been used by relatively few people in the past due to the very high cost. Someone once calculated that the cost of downloading 20 gigabytes of music or videos would cost more than buying a typical house! The providers of mobile Internet services have had to drastically reduce their prices in order to become more competitive with alternative methods, and the cost is now more in line with these alternatives.

There are obvious attractions to a form of Internet access that can be used at home or on the move. In fact it can be used anywhere that a suitably strong signal can be obtained. Bear in mind though, that it is less than ideal if you can not obtain a good signal when using the Internet at home, because a weak or mediocre signal will give a relatively slow connection speed. Sharing this type of interconnection can be difficult, and might not be permitted by the ISP. While downloading large amounts of data via this type of connection is far less expensive than it used to be, it could still be relatively expensive.

Index